MW00899132

WINDOWS FILE MANAGEMENT

MADE EASY

Take Control of Your Files and Folders

By James Bernstein

Copyright © 2021 by James Bernstein. All rights reserved.

All rights reserved. This book or any portion thereof
may not be reproduced or used in any manner whatsoever
without the express written permission of the publisher
except for the use of brief quotations in a book review.

Printed in the United States of America

Bernstein, James
Windows File Management Made Easy
Part of the Windows Made Easy series

For more information on reproducing sections of this book or sales of this book,
go to **www.madeeasybookseries.com**

Contents

Introduction

If you use a computer at home or at work on a regular basis then you should be familiar with the concept of files and folders and how you have both of them stored on the hard drive of your desktop or laptop, and without access to these files and folders it's hard to get your work done.

Knowing how to manage these files and folders is essential if you want to become a proficient computer user and if you can't easily find them or know how to properly maniple them, then becoming a so called computer expert will not be possible. You would be surprised at how many people are really skilled at using programs like Excel or Photoshop yet can't find their files when they need them.

Once you learn the basics of how the Windows file structure works and how to do things like copy files and search for files and folders on your computer, you will realize how it makes almost all of your other computer tasks easier. Since almost every program you use involves opening files except for maybe using your web browser, it's essential to know where your files and folders are located and what files are associated with which program.

The goal of this book is to make you a file managing expert without confusing you in the process. I will go through the material step by step and keep things simple while providing you with the information you need to be able to master the topics at hand. Even though the subject of this book is fairly specific, there is still a lot of information to cover. So on that note let's start showing our files and folders who's the boss!

Chapter 1 – Why You Need to Know How to Manage Your Files

Like I mentioned in the Introduction, in order to be a proficient computer expert you will need to know how to manage your files and how the Windows file system works. And if you ever want to become a computer expert... or geek, then you definitely need to know how to do this.

Let's say you are doing something fairly simple such as typing up a resume using Microsoft Word. When you are finished or when you get to a stopping point you will need to save your work otherwise you will have done all that work for nothing. If you don't know anything about how your files and folders are stored you might just end up saving it wherever Word decides that it will save your files. In most cases, this will be your *Documents* folder on your hard drive under your user profile folder.

Word will also come up with a name for the document based on the text you have at the beginning of the document so if you don't change it the first time you save it then you might have trouble finding it later on since the name of the document might not match what the document is about. And yes, knowing how to name your files is part of the file management process.

If you would like to learn more about Microsoft Word and the other programs that come with Microsoft Office then check out my book called **Office Made Easy**.
https://www.amazon.com/dp/1729013732

Now let's say you want to email your resume to your future employer as an attachment to the email. If you don't know what it's called or know where you saved it then accomplishing this task will be quite difficult. But if you know how to search for a Word file created on a certain date then it shouldn't be too hard to find your resume so you can send it off to your new boss.

When you are looking at this resume Word document on your computer you might notice that the file ends with **.docx** and you might be wondering what that means. So if you saved your file with the name *Resume* then Windows will put the file extension .docx at the end so the actual file name will be **Resume.docx**. Knowing that any file with .docx on the end is a Microsoft Word file will be helpful when browsing your files and especially when searching for your files. I will be covering file extensions later in this book.

Now let's say you have a bunch of pictures on your smartphone that you want to transfer over to your computer to either free up space on your phone or store them in both locations so your computer will act as a backup. Knowing the difference between copying files and moving files is essential here because if you want to accomplish either task, you will need to know how to do each one of these procedures.

Another situation might involve having the need to delete a bunch of files because you no longer need them or need to free up space on your hard drive. If you didn't know any better you might think you might have to delete them one by one and if you have hundreds of files, or even thousands of them then this will take a considerable amount of time. Lucky for us we can delete files in bulk as well as copy and move them in bulk.

When you do delete these files you won't get your hard drive space back because they will end up in the *Recycle Bin* until you manually delete them from the "trash" to get your free space back. The Recycle Bin will be discussed in more detail later in this book.

I can go on and on with different scenarios that involve knowing how to properly manage your files and folders, but you should have a pretty good idea by now that it's something you really need to know how to do if you want to be an effective computer user. Even if you don't use Windows but rather a Mac or even Linux, you will still need to be able to manage your files and folders, although the process will vary between operating systems.

Topics Covered In This Book
You wouldn't think there was much to file and folder management in Windows or with any operating system, but you would be surprised how much there is to know about the subject. Sure you can get along just fine knowing the basics but why not take a little extra time to learn some of the more advanced topics and make yourself more of an expert? Once you really know the ins and outs of file and folder management it makes troubleshooting your computer issues so much easier.

There will be many topics discussed in this book and some of them will be very detailed discussions and others more simplified based on how much you really need to know about the particular subject. As you go through the chapters you will see what kind of material will be covered but for now I just wanted to give you a general idea of all the fun stuff you have to look forward to! Here is a listing of many of the topics I will be covering in this book.

- The Windows file structure
- Changing folder options
- Creating file and folder shortcuts
- Creating files and folders
- Copying, moving, deleting and renaming files and folders
- Searching for files and folders
- File extensions
- Backups
- Windows default folders
- User folders
- File associations
- File Explorer (aka Windows Explorer)
- Resizing photo file sizes for emailing etc.
- The Recycle Bin
- Copying files from your smartphone to your computer
- Viewing and changing file and folder permissions
- Sharing files and folders

Chapter 2 – The Windows File System

As with most technology related topics, you often have some key subjects that you need to master first before moving on to some of the other related topics. And in my opinion, knowing how the Windows file system works is a key topic you should be very familiar with before moving on to other aspects relating to Windows file management.

File Systems Explained
You might be asking yourself, what do you mean by the Windows file system? Or, what exactly is a file system? Well I'm glad you asked! A file system often is used to control how data is stored and retrieved from your hard drive. You might have heard the people talking about 1's and 0's relating to how data is stored on a computer. If computers didn't have file systems then they wouldn't know where one section of data began or where one ended and all our files would be lumped together into one giant chunk or unusable data. But thanks to file systems, our computer can separate this data into individual files that are stored in directories (or folders) allowing us to use and manipulate this data.

Current versions of Windows use the NTFS (New Technology File System) file system which has been in use since 1993 and started with Windows NT 3.1. NTFS was not always the default file system for desktop versions of Windows, but it has been since Windows XP back in 2001. Before that, Windows used the FAT32 file system for Windows 95 and 98.

There are a lot of differences between FAT32 and NTFS such as NFTS supporting much larger hard drives and also offering higher security features and encryption capabilities. FAT32 is still commonly used with flash drives and other smaller drives. If you right click on your hard drive and choose *Properties* you will see the file system that is being used on that drive. Figure 2.1 shows an NTFS formatted hard drive on the left and a FAT32 formatted flash drive on the right.

One thing you might have noticed when it comes to Windows 10 is that Microsoft is constantly changing how you do things and how you get to certain tools etc. so if something is not where it should be, that is most likely thanks to a Windows update.

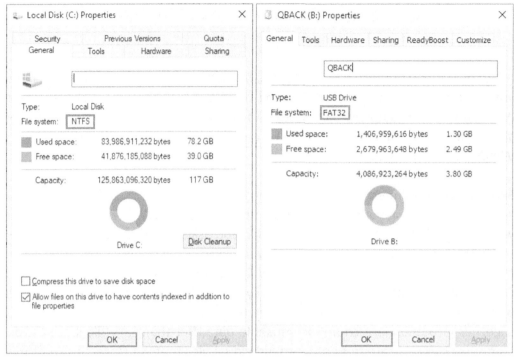

Figure 2.1

File Explorer (aka Windows Explorer)

The main tool that you will be using to manage your files and folders within Windows is called File Explorer. In older versions of Windows you will see it be called Windows Explorer. This tool allows you to see all of the files and folders on your hard drive and is used to do things such as copy files, open files, check file properties, create folders and so on.

There are several ways to open File explorer such as clicking on the Windows System folder from your Start menu and then selecting the File Explorer icon from the list as shown in figure 2.2. You can also right click the Start button and choose Windows Explorer even though I'm not sure why they have a different name when using this method. You can also use the keyboard shortcut *Windows Key + E* to open File explorer without using a mouse. The Windows key is generally to the right of the *Ctrl* key on the left side of your keyboard.

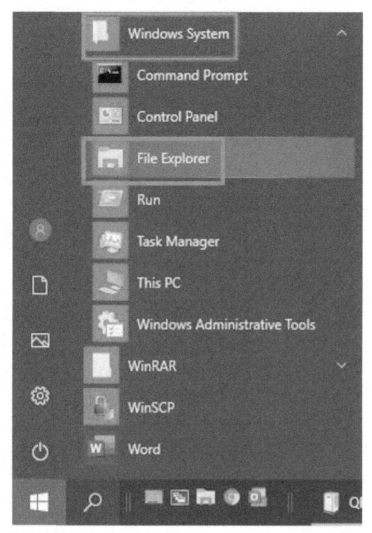

Figure 2.2

Once you have File Explorer open you will be shown any hard drives, flash drives, DVD drives and so on that are installed on your computer. Figure 2.3 shows the File Explorer program open on my computer and it's focused on the C drive of my computer. The C drive is usually where Windows and any programs are installed on your computer. Most home computers will come with just one hard drive while others might have more than one. You can add additional hard drives to your computer if you need to add more storage space.

As you can see from figure 2.3, there are several components to the File Explorer tool, and I will be going into these features in more detail throughout this book. You can also see that there is a left and right pane separated by a scroll bar. It is important to understand how these panes work and the information they show you. If you click on a folder in the left pane, it will show you the contents of that folder on the right pane. Figure 2.4 shows an example that is a little easier to see compared to figure 2.3.

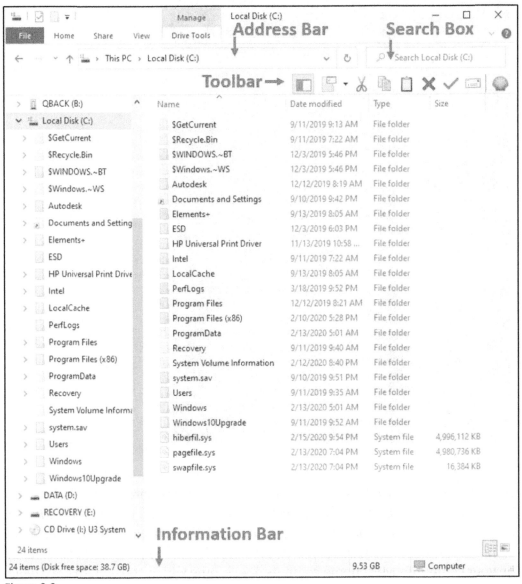

Figure 2.3

On the left you can see there is a folder called *Photos* and when I click on that it expands the Photos folder to show the other folders and the one file that is contained in that folder on the right. Figure 2.5 shows that you can also click on the Photos folder on the left and have it show those same subfolders in the right pane as well but notice how it doesn't show the *Mountains.jpg* file. You will only be able to see folders on the left, but you can see folders AND files on the right.

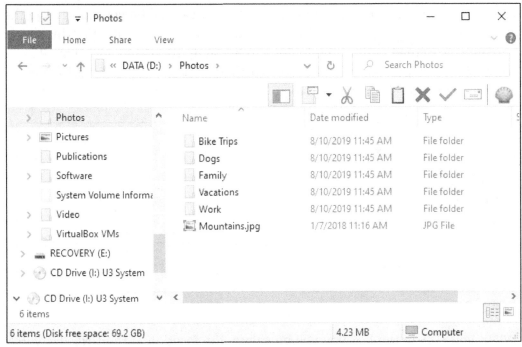

Figure 2.4

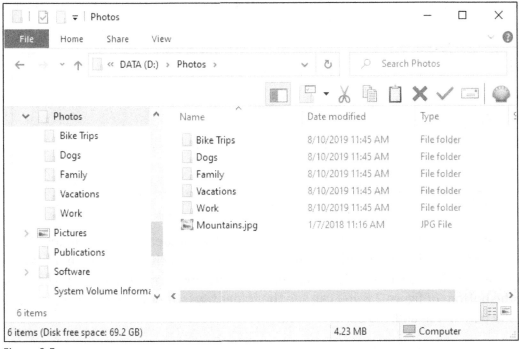

Figure 2.5

Looking back at figure 2.3 you will see there is a section labeled *Address Bar*. Here you will be shown the location on your hard drive that you are working in. There are two ways to view the location in the address bar. When you don't have the mouse cursor in the box you will see the view as shown in figure 2.6. This shows you an easy to read path to the folder you are in. In this case I am on my PC in a folder called Photos on my D drive which is a secondary hard drive on my computer separate from my C drive.

Figure 2.6

When you click in the box you will be shown the location in the UNC (Universal Naming Convention) path format which is commonly used to show the path for folders stored on networked drives. Figure 2.7 shows the same location as seen in figure 2.6 but using the UNC format.

Figure 2.7

Figure 2.8 shows a folder location for another folder that has many more subfolders, or levels than the example in figure 2.7. Each part of the path that is separated by a backslash (\) indicates a separate subfolder of the prior folder. At the bottom of figure 2.8 you can see the folder tree structure that corresponds to the path in the address bar.

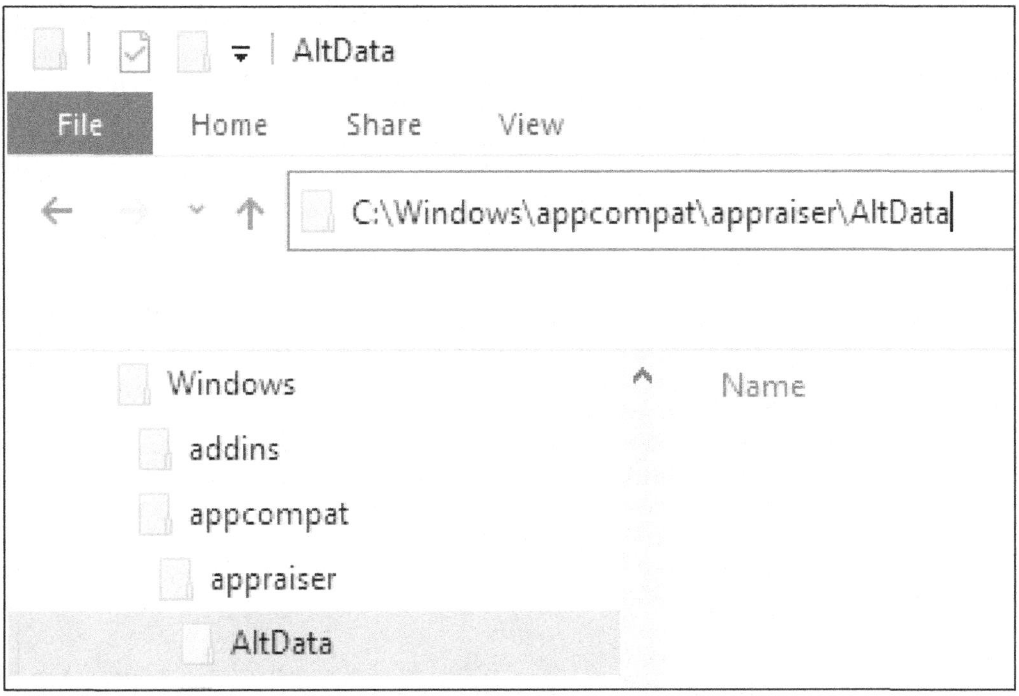

Figure 2.8

Now that you have seen folder paths in action, I want to take a moment to discuss the tree structure that Windows and most other operating systems use to organize their folders. The folders on your computer will be organized in a tree structure with folders being housed within folders that can span many levels. If you have ever seen an organization chart then it looks very similar.

Figure 2.9 shows the main folder which is called the root drive, and this is the top of the folder tree. Within this folder you will have other folders such as Folder A and Folder B. Then within Folder A and Folder B you can have another layer of folders. Any folder that is contained within another folder is called a *subfolder*. So Folder A is a subfolder of the Root folder and Subfolder A is a subfolder of Folder A.

These folders and subfolders are what make the path to a folder or file. So the path to *Subfolder A2* would look like this. **C:\Folder B\Subfolder A\Subfolder A2**. You will usually see the root folder of a drive labeled with its drive letter followed by a colon (C:).

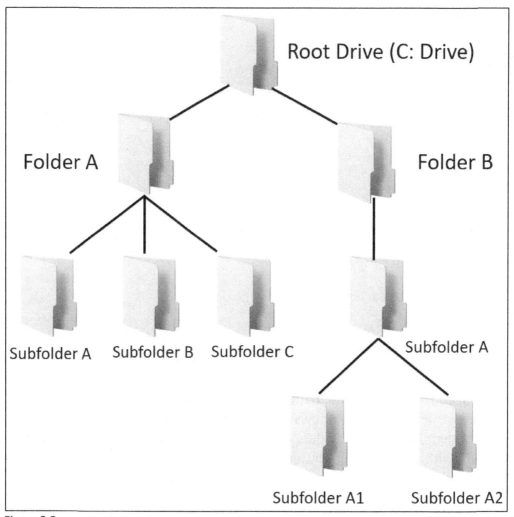

Figure 2.9

I have created the folder structure that I just discussed, and the results are shown in figure 2.10. Figure 2.11 shows the folder path in the UNC format which will be displayed when you click inside the address box.

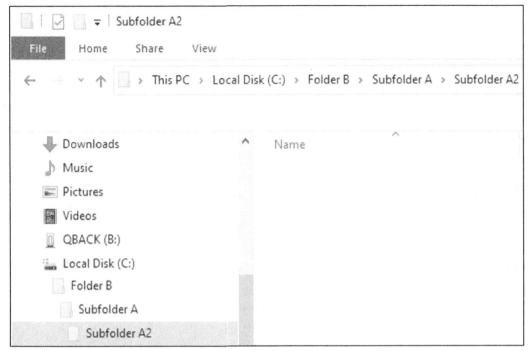

Figure 2.10

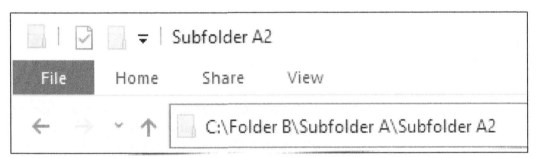

Figure 2.11

Since I will be going over items from the File Explorer toolbar and search box later on in the book I will now focus on the status bar at the bottom of the window. This section of File Explorer is used to give you information about the current file(s) or folder(s) you have selected.

Figure 2.12 shows a folder called *SLO – 6-19* under a folder called *Mountain Biking* which is in the Windows default *Pictures* folder. As you can see at the bottom left it shows that there are 42 items (or pictures in this case) in this folder and over to the right it tells me that the size of these 42 pictures is 15.6 MB. It also shows me that I have 69.2 GB free space on the drive that contains these pictures which in this case is the C drive.

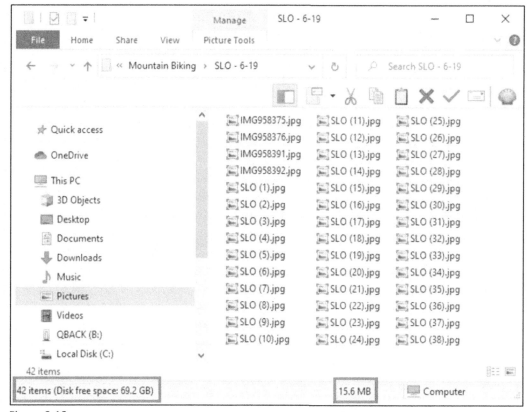

Figure 2.12

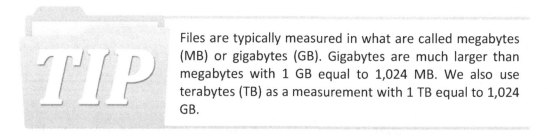

Files are typically measured in what are called megabytes (MB) or gigabytes (GB). Gigabytes are much larger than megabytes with 1 GB equal to 1,024 MB. We also use terabytes (TB) as a measurement with 1 TB equal to 1,024 GB.

One thing to be aware of when using the status bar is that the size of the items shown might not be the real size of the items in that folder. For example, let's say I add a new folder called *Additional Photos* as a subfolder to the SLO – 6-19 folder and place a bunch of new photos in that folder.

As you can see in figure 2.13 that the item count went from 42 to 43 because of the addition of this new folder but the size is still showing 15.6 MB. This is because File Explorer will only show the size of the files within the folder and won't include the size of the files within any subfolders that may exist.

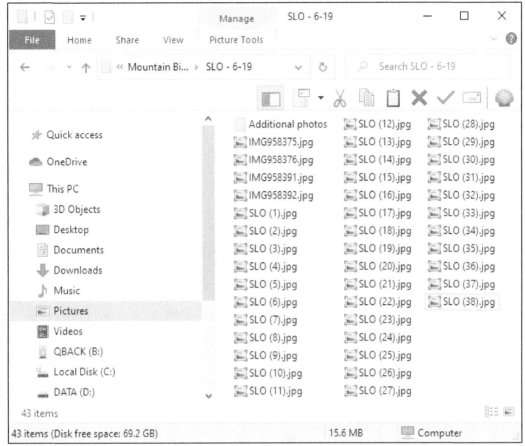

Figure 2.13

If I were to highlight all the contents of the SLO – 6-19 folder, right click on them and choose *Properties*, I would be shown the real file count and size of all the files included in the SLO – 6-19 folder as shown in figure 2.14. As you can see it shows 83 files rather than 42 and 1 folder (Additional Photos folder) and that the size of everything is 31.3 MB rather than 15.6 MB as the status bar shows in figure 2.13.

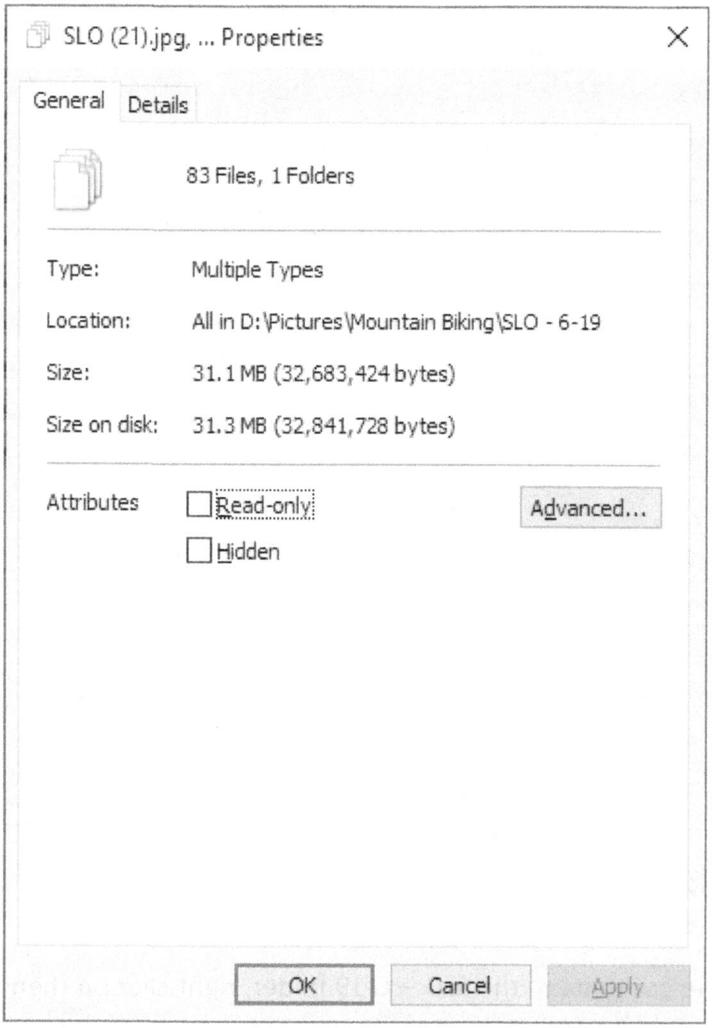

Figure 2.14

Understanding how to use File Explorer is essential if you want to be proficient with Windows file management and I will be using File Explorer throughout this book which should help you get a handle on it. Hopefully, as you follow along you will become more comfortable using it and any stress that you feel from having to use it eventually disappears.

View Options
Now that you have seen how File Explorer works and have realized that you will be using it on a regular basis you might want to know how you can change the way your files and folders are viewed within the tool to make things easier to see and work with.

There are several ways to view the contents of your computer while using File Explorer and even when doing something like opening or saving a file from a program such as Microsoft Word. Now when I refer to changing views, I mean the way files and folders are displayed on the screen and what information you see or don't see next to them.

Windows has some default views when you open folders that contain certain types of files. For example, when you open your Pictures folder, Windows likes to display the files as icons (or thumbnails) since they are pictures. This makes it easier to see what each image file is without having to open each one up individually. Figure 2.15 shows the same SLO – 6-19 folder we have been working with set to be viewed as icons. By using this view I can get a preview of each picture to see which ones I want to open, copy, delete and so on.

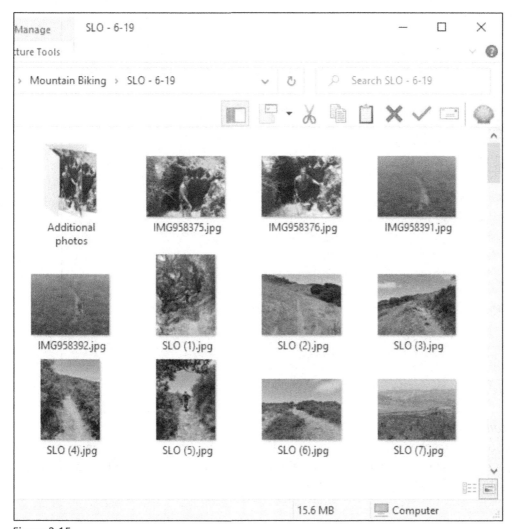

Figure 2.15

Now I would like to take a moment to go over all the choices you have for your folder views and show some examples of each type.

List
This view shows you only the files and folders with their associated names.

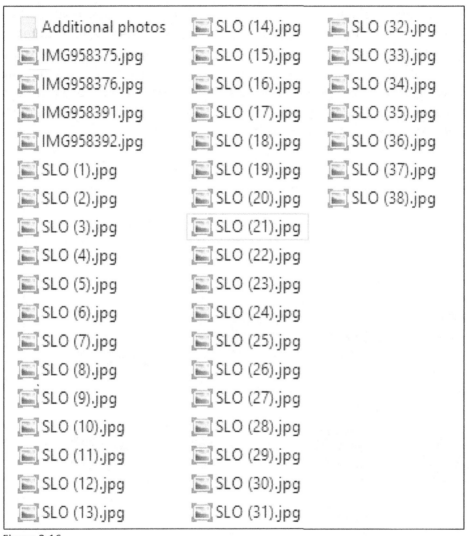

Figure 2.16

Details
If you need to see information such as the date the file or folder was created, its type or file size you can use the Details view. This will display the files and folders in columns rather than just as a list.

Name	Date	Type	Size
Additional photos	2/18/2020 12:22 PM	File folder	
IMG958375.jpg	6/17/2019 4:12 PM	JPG File	87 KB
IMG958376.jpg	6/17/2019 4:12 PM	JPG File	75 KB
IMG958391.jpg	6/17/2019 4:12 PM	JPG File	129 KB
IMG958392.jpg	6/17/2019 4:12 PM	JPG File	133 KB
SLO (1).jpg	6/15/2019 11:40 AM	JPG File	587 KB
SLO (2).jpg	6/15/2019 11:49 AM	JPG File	473 KB
SLO (3).jpg	6/15/2019 11:51 AM	JPG File	410 KB
SLO (4).jpg	6/15/2019 12:18 PM	JPG File	509 KB
SLO (5).jpg	6/15/2019 12:19 PM	JPG File	525 KB
SLO (6).jpg	6/15/2019 12:29 PM	JPG File	417 KB
SLO (7).jpg	6/15/2019 12:33 PM	JPG File	349 KB
SLO (8).jpg	6/15/2019 12:34 PM	JPG File	640 KB
SLO (9).jpg	6/15/2019 12:35 PM	JPG File	439 KB
SLO (10).jpg	6/15/2019 12:46 PM	JPG File	625 KB
SLO (11).jpg	6/15/2019 12:47 PM	JPG File	523 KB

Figure 2.17

Windows uses some default column types based on what type of files you are looking on but it's fairly easy to add additional columns for other types of details. To do so simply right click on any of the column names and choose one of the other categories or you can click on *More* to get a complete listing of the detail types to choose from as shown in figure 2.18 You can also use the *Move Up* and *Move Down* buttons to change the order of the columns.

When in Details view you can use your mouse to drag and drop the location of the columns to easily arrange their order rather than using the right click and choosing More option as described above.

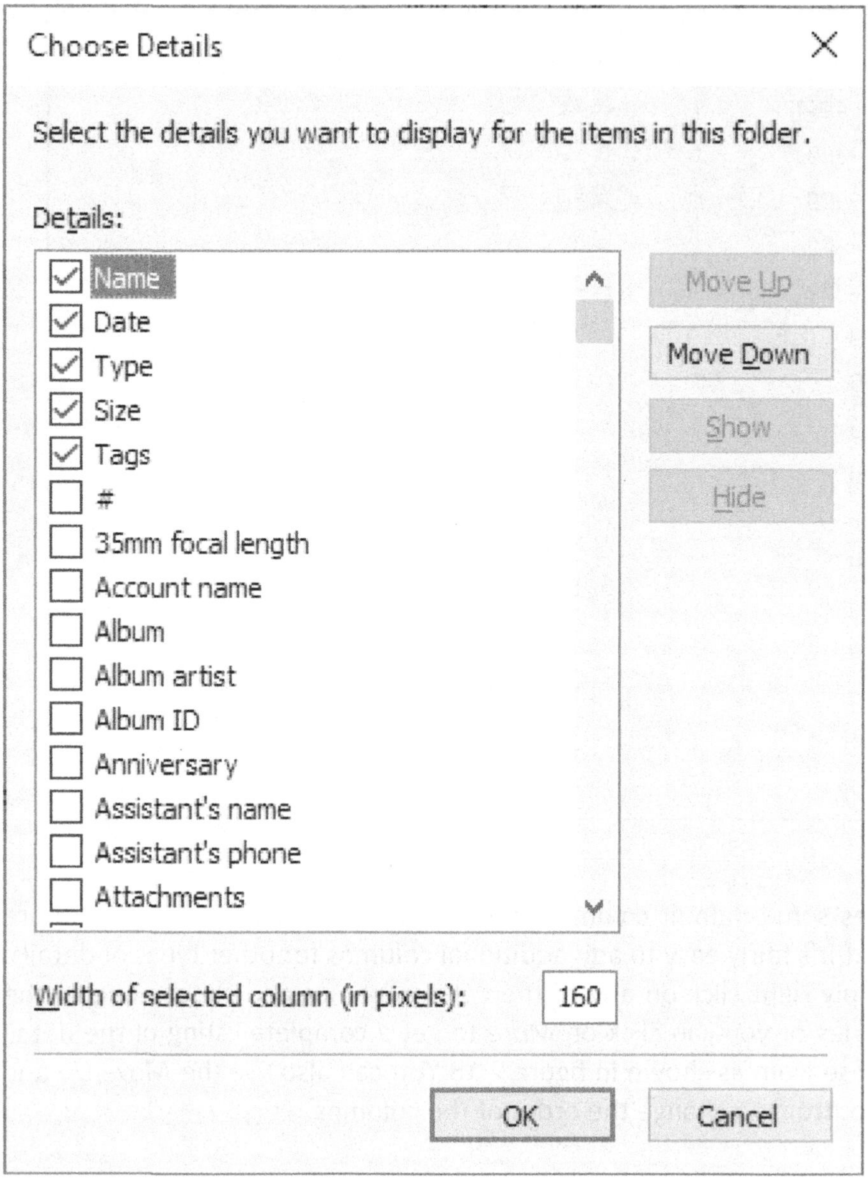

Figure 2.18

Small, Medium and Large Icons
I showed an example of Large Icons back in figure 2.15 and there are other sizes to choose from when using the icons setting which will show a thumbnail preview of the file. This view won't show a preview for certain types of files such as documents and system files but will rather just show a larger icon in its place as shown in figure 2.19.

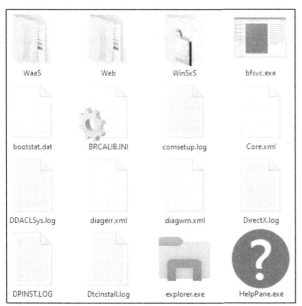

Figure 2.19

Tiles

This view is similar to the Icon view but shows the information for the files and folders next to them rather than below them.

Figure 2.20

Content

This view is sort of like a combination of the Tiles and Details view where you will see a small thumbnail but also get some information about each file and folder next to them.

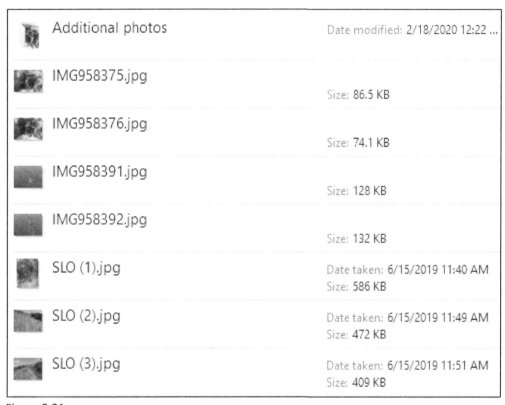

Figure 2.21

To change the views in File Explorer you can go to the *View* tab and then choose the view that you want to use under the *Layout* section.

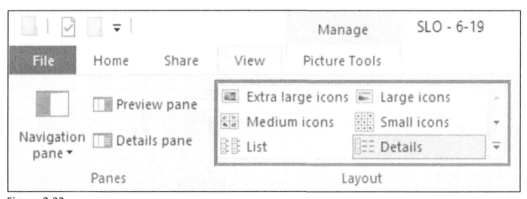

Figure 2.22

If you look at the left of figure 2.22 you will see choice *Preview pane* and *Details pane*. These views can be used to show you additional information for your files and folders so I would try them out and see how they work for you. If you don't like the view it gives you, simply click the icon again to have it changed back. Figure 2.23 shows an example of what you see when using the Preview pane and figure 2.24 shows how the Details pane looks when selected. These views work great for things like pictures or movies where you can see a preview but won't do you much good for other types of files such as documents or spreadsheets.

Figure 2.23

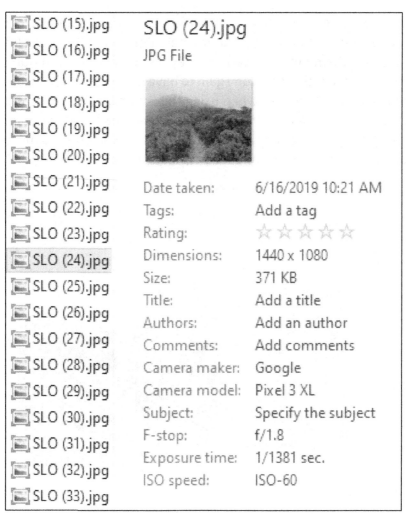

Figure 2.24

One other section from the View tab I want to discuss is the *Current view* area. Here you can quickly change how your files and folders are viewed such as sorting them by name or date or grouping them by file type or size etc.

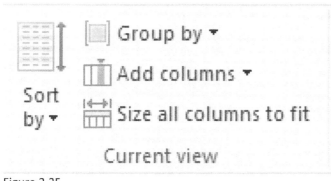

Figure 2.25

The *Add columns* option will allow you to add additional columns when using the Details view which I went over earlier in this section. The *Size all columns to fit* option will resize the width of all of the columns you are using so they fit the names of the files without having too much extra space in between them. If any of these options are greyed out that means you are not using a view that can be manipulated by using one of these view choices.

File Extensions and Associations
When working with your files you have most likely noticed that certain files have specific letters after the name of the file. For example, you might have noticed that pictures often have .jpg on the end of them or that text files end in .txt.

File extensions are used to tell Windows what program to open a certain type of file with. If they weren't used, then every time you double clicked a file you would be asked what program you wanted to open it with, and if you didn't know what type of file it was, then that would make things very difficult. File extensions are hidden by default in Windows (with a few exceptions). I will be going over how to "unhide" these file extensions later in Chapter 5.

A file extension consists of a period followed by three or more letters (or sometimes numbers) afterward denoting what program the file is to be associated with. For example, with a file called **resume.docx,** the file name is **resume** and the extension is **.docx,** and **.docx** is the file extension associated with Microsoft Word. So, when you double click the resume.docx file, Windows knows to open it with Microsoft Word. However, if you don't have Microsoft Word installed, it won't know what to open it with because Word will register that extension with Windows only after you install it on the computer.

You should not try to change the file extension on a file because it will cause that file to lose its association with the program that is used to open that type of file. It will also lose its icon or thumbnail view when you go to look at it in File Explorer as seen in figure 2.26. Or if you change the file extension to that for another program then Windows will change the icon to match whatever icon is associated with that particular program.

Figure 2.26

If you change a file extension and then go to open that file, Windows will give you a message asking you how you want to open the file if it doesn't have that file extension registered. Most of the time it will give you a listing of programs it thinks might be able to open the file and also a choice to browse for other programs or apps.

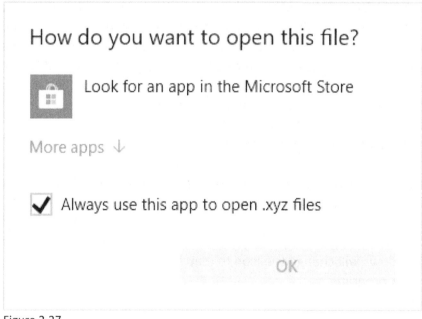

Figure 2.27

If you have a need to, you can try to open one type of file with another program other than the one the file extension is associated with by right clicking on the file and choosing *Open With* and selecting a different program from the list.

Chapter 3 – Windows Default Folders

When you install Microsoft Windows, the setup process will create its own file structure and place files and folders on your hard drive in the appropriate locations so that things work the way they should. In fact, if you try and change or delete certain default files or folders then you will find that Windows will stop working altogether so it's a good idea to know the basics about these default folders and what you can and can't do with them.

Windows Default Storage Folders
Throughout the years, Microsoft has included a variety of default, or built in folders for storing different types of files such as documents, pictures, music, videos and so on since these are the most commonly used types of files for many people.

You might have noticed when you go to save something like a Word document that it defaults to the *Documents* folder or if you go to set a different desktop background image for your computer that it will default to the *Pictures* folder. This is just Microsoft trying to make things easy on us and keep things consistent for people who use Windows. It is kind of a good idea because if you need to work on someone else's computer and need to find where they saved a certain spreadsheet for example, then there is a good chance that it is in that person's Documents folder. It also forces users to keep files of certain types in these folders to keep things organized.

Of course you don't need to use these default folders if you don't want to and can save and store your files wherever you like on your computer. I have a secondary hard drive in my computer where I store all of my personal files and I do this because it keeps them away from the operating system. This way if Windows crashes or I get a virus that affects Windows or my C drive then there is a much better chance that my personal files will be unaffected, and I can just format my C drive and reinstall Windows without worrying about losing my files.

If you open Windows Explorer and click on *This PC* you will see most of these default folders over in the right hand pane as seen in figure 3.1. You will also see them listed below This PC in the left hand pane. Then all you need to do is double click on a particular folder to see the files contained within that folder.

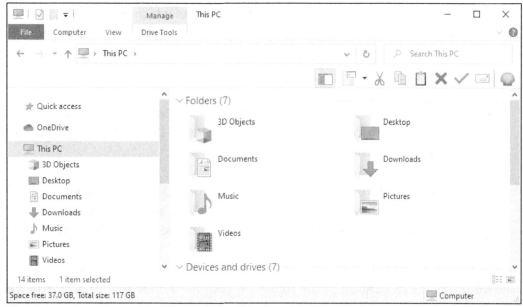

Figure 3.1

The Documents, Music, Videos and Pictures folders should be pretty self-explanatory so now I will discuss the other folders seen in figure 3.1 plus the other default folders that come with Windows that are not shown.

- **3D Objects** – This is used to save files from Paint 3D which is the more improved and modern version of the old school Paint program.

- **Desktop** – Many people like to keep files and folders on their desktop and this folder is the actual location where these files and folders are kept. If you look at the contents of this folder and then at your actual desktop, you will notice that they are exactly the same.

- **Downloads** – When you download files from the Internet, Windows will want to put them in this folder by default. That way if you need to find a file after you have downloaded it you can easily find it by looking here.

- **Contacts** – This is used for storing personal contact information for other people that can be used with programs such as Windows Fax and Scan

- **Favorites** – When you save favorites (or bookmarks) in the Internet Explorer web browser, they are saved here. Internet Explorer has now been replaced by the Edge web browser in Windows 10even though it's still possible to use Internet Explorer (for now).

- **Links** – Links was used to place the shortcuts which were pinned to the Favorites section in previous versions of Windows which was replaced with Quick Access in Windows 10. I will be discussing the Quick Access section in Chapter 7.

- **Saved Games** – This is used to save game information for Windows games and some Microsoft games. It most likely won't be used to save any third party game information.

- **Searches** – Here you will find information about locations on your computer that have been indexed for searching and also any saved search information. I will be going over searching for files and folders in chapter

If you right click on one of these folders and then click on *Properties*, you will be shown the physical location of the folder on your hard drive (figure 3.2). You will also be shown how many files and folders it contains as well as the size of those files and folders. You will notice that all of these folders are under *C:\Users* and I will be discussing the Users folder in the next section.

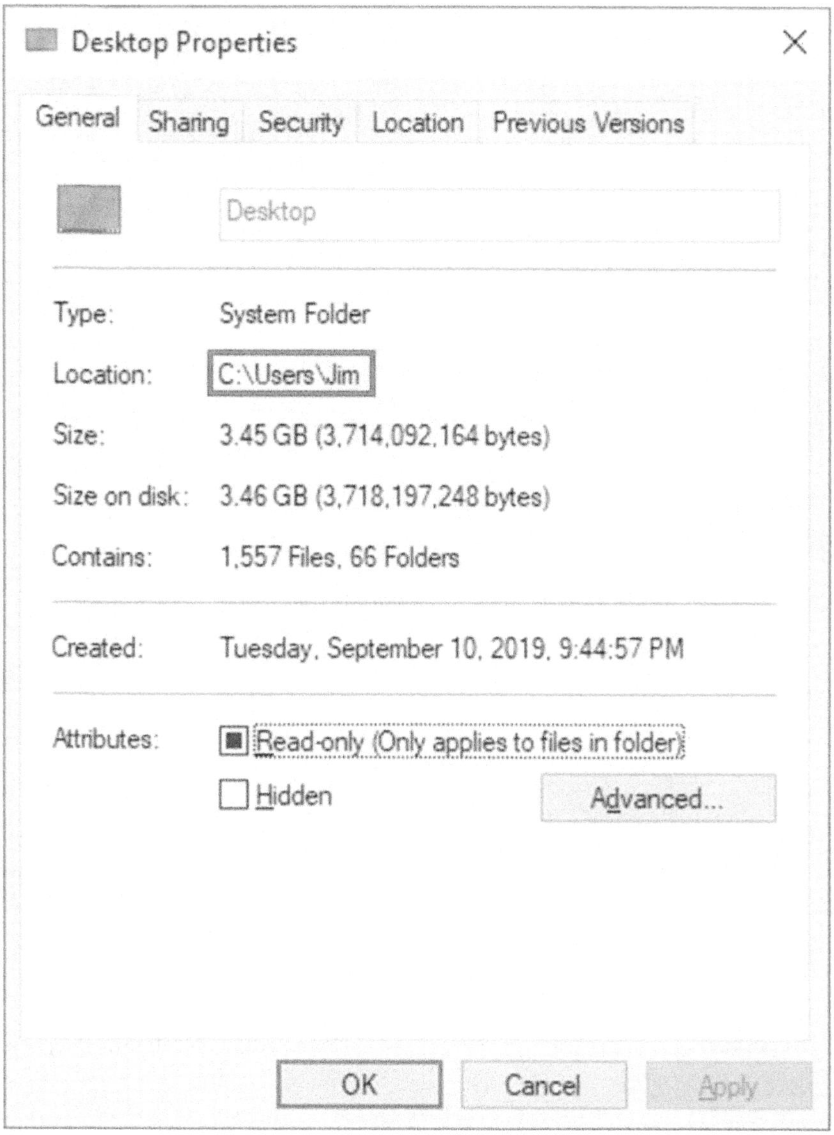

Figure 3.2

One thing I wanted to mention even though it's a more advanced topic is that you can change the physical location of these folders while still retaining their functionality. You might remember me mentioning that I kept my documents on my other hard drive. To help me do this, I changed the location of the Documents folder from *C:\User\Jim\Documents* to *D:\My Documents* by specifying a new location from the Location tab as seen in figure 3.3.

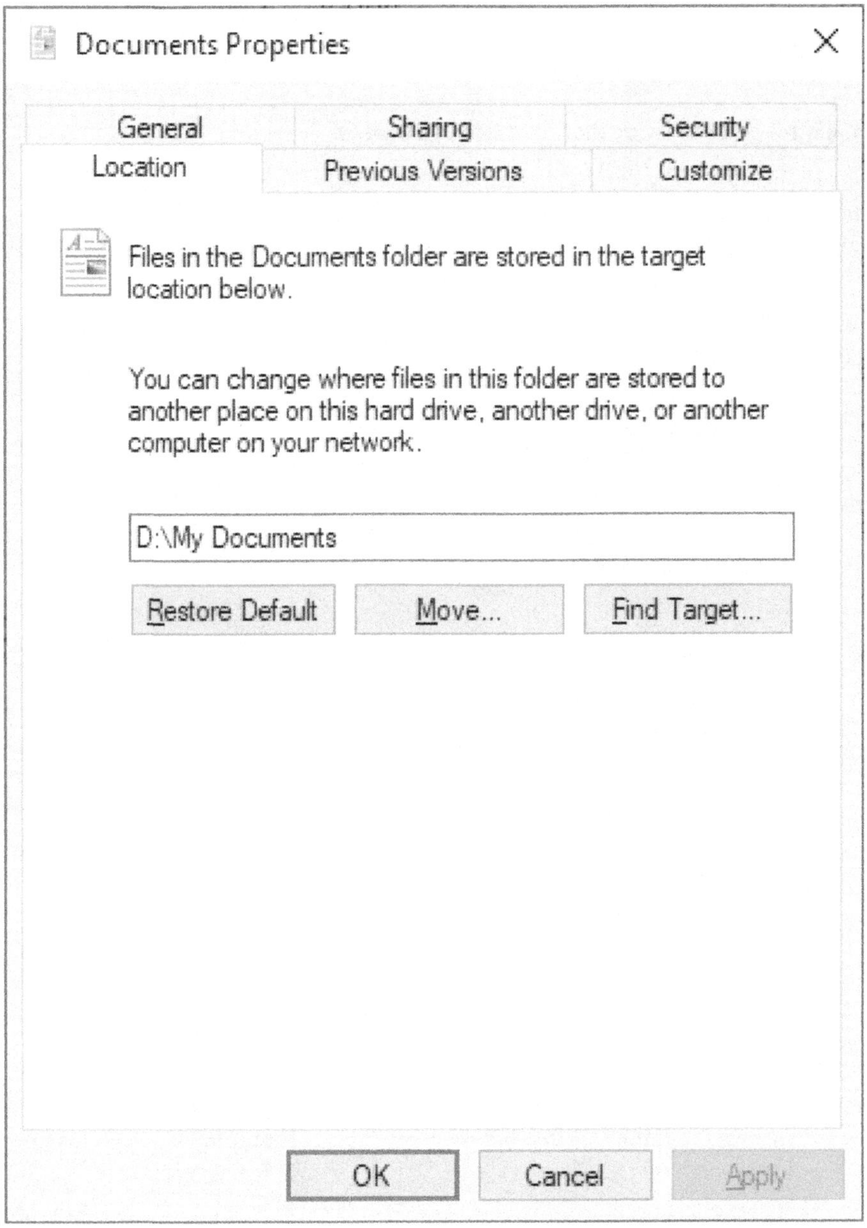

Figure 3.3

If you think you might want to customize where your files are kept by default just be sure to come up with a plan that will let you keep things organized and allow you to easily find the files you are looking for.

Users Folder

Whenever you boot up your computer you are prompted to log into your user account with a name and password to get into your computer. If you share your computer with other people then they might each have their own user account that they use to log in with. Since Windows allows multiple users to be configured on the same computer, it needs to be able to keep all of these user's files in order and separate from other users. This is where the *Users* folder comes into play.

The Users folder is located at the root of the system drive or C drive. The drive that Windows is installed on is often referred to as the *system drive.* Back in older versions of Windows, you would find your personal files under *Documents and Settings.*

You can install Windows on a different drive if you really wanted to, but by default it will be installed on the C drive and it's probably a good idea to keep it this way to avoid issues down the road.

As you can see in figure 3.4, this computer has four user accounts configured on it and each one has its own username folder under the main Users folder.

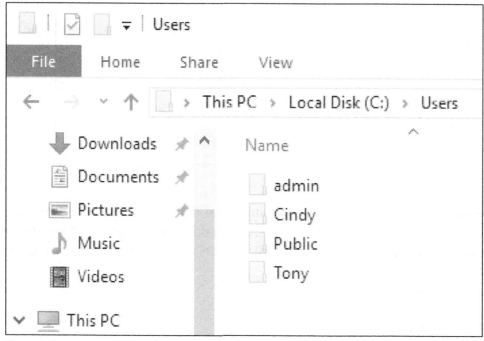

Figure 3.4

If I were to double click on a username folder such as Tony you can see that it has all of the default Windows folders that I just discussed listed underneath the username folder which shows you that Windows will want to keep all of your personal files in one place under this Users folder.

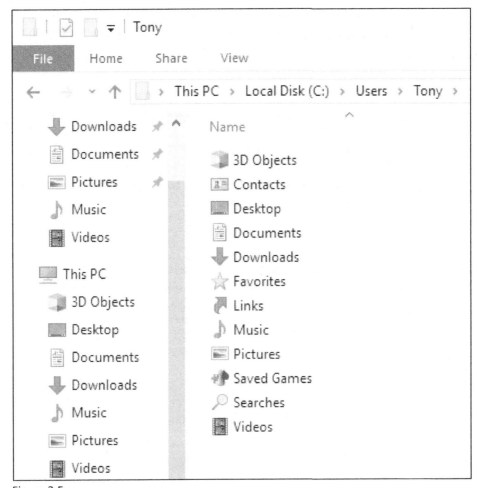

Figure 3.5

If your user account does not have administrator rights then you will not be able to get into any of the other Users folders. This is done on purpose so that you can keep your personal files and folders secure when sharing a computer with other people.

Program Files Folders

Another set of folders I wanted to discuss because you might need to access these for troubleshooting are the Program Files folders. These are used to store the files needed for programs installed on your computer. Keep in mind that not all of the files for your installed programs go here since most software installs files in the Windows folder as well (discussed next).

If you open File Explorer and click on your system drive (C: drive) then you will notice that there are two Program Files folders with one of them having (x86) after it.

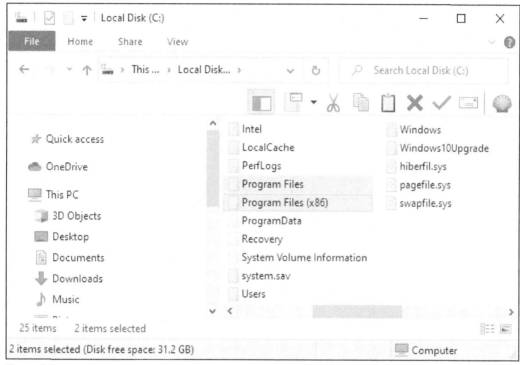

Figure 3.6

This is because some software is 32 bit, and some is 64 bit. When you hear someone talking about 32 or 64 bit software, they are referring to how much data can be transferred and at what speed. Older versions of Windows were 32 bit so you could only run 32 bit software on them. Newer versions of Windows are 64 bit and can run 32 bit and 64 bit software. The processor in your computer has to be 64 bit to run a 64 bit version of Windows which all processors these days are. The folder that is called *Program Files (x86)* is where 32 bit software is installed.

When you install new software, Windows will know which one of these folders to install the software into based on the installation file. When you have a choice to install software, you usually want to choose the 64 bit version unless you are on an older version of Windows. If you try and install 64 bit software on a 32 bit version of Windows, the installation will fail, and you will be told that your computer will not support the software you are trying to install.

Knowing where your software is installed comes in handy if you ever need to see where some software is installed or even need to find out if some software is even installed for example. You can right click on any of your program's icons to see where the software is installed. Just look in the *Target* box to see the path to the executable. The executable is the file that is used to run the program and usually ends in **.exe**. I will be discussing shortcuts in Chapter 4 which should make this a little clearer if it's kind of confusing for you at the moment.

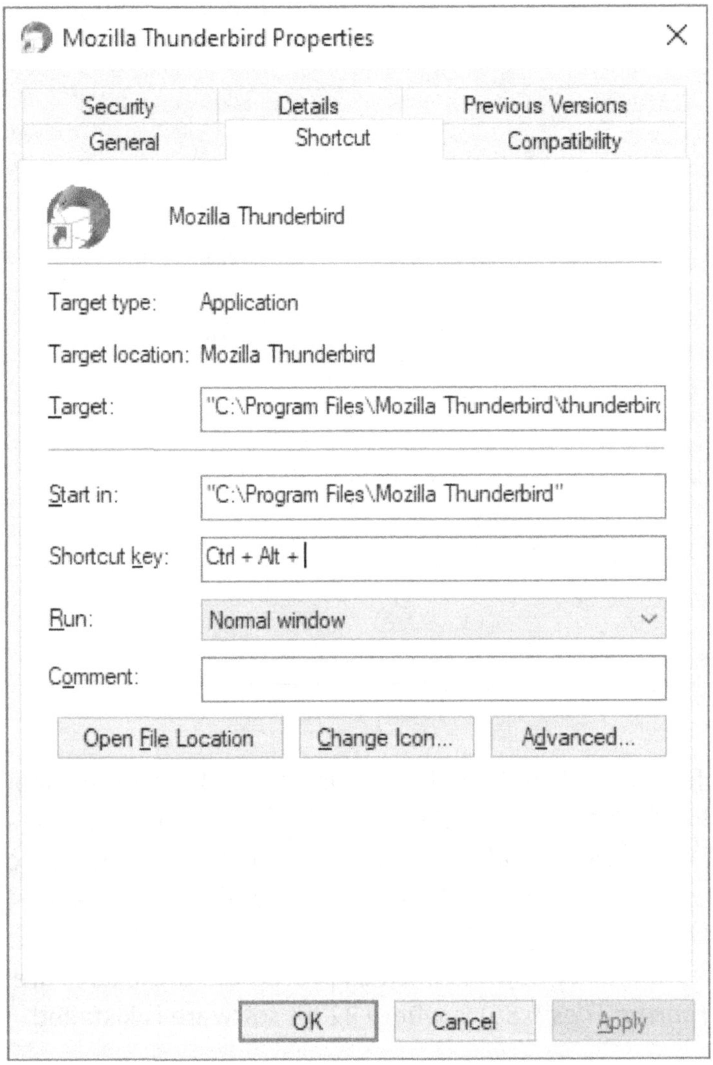

Figure 3.7

The Windows Operating System Folder

The last default folder I want to cover is the Windows folder itself. There are many more default folders on your computer, but this book is not about Windows but rather the files and folders contained within Windows. With that being the case, it's still a good idea to have an idea of what types of files and folders you will find within the Windows folder.

If you would like to learn more about how Windows 10 operates and make yourself more proficient with the Windows operating system then check out my book called **Windows 10 Made Easy**.
https://www.amazon.com/dp/1082480916

The Windows folder is where Windows is installed and where its supporting files are placed. There are many files and subfolders under the main Windows folder which is located in the root of your system drive (C:) as you can see in figure 3.8.

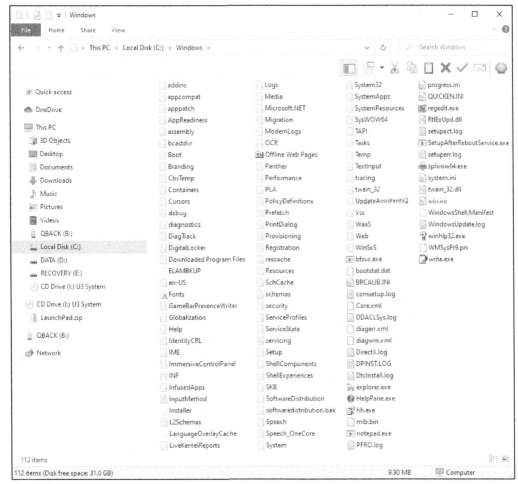

Figure 3.8

If you were to right click on the Windows folder itself and then choose Properties you would be able to see exactly how many files and subfolders are in this folder. Of course the numbers you see will not be exactly the same as mine.

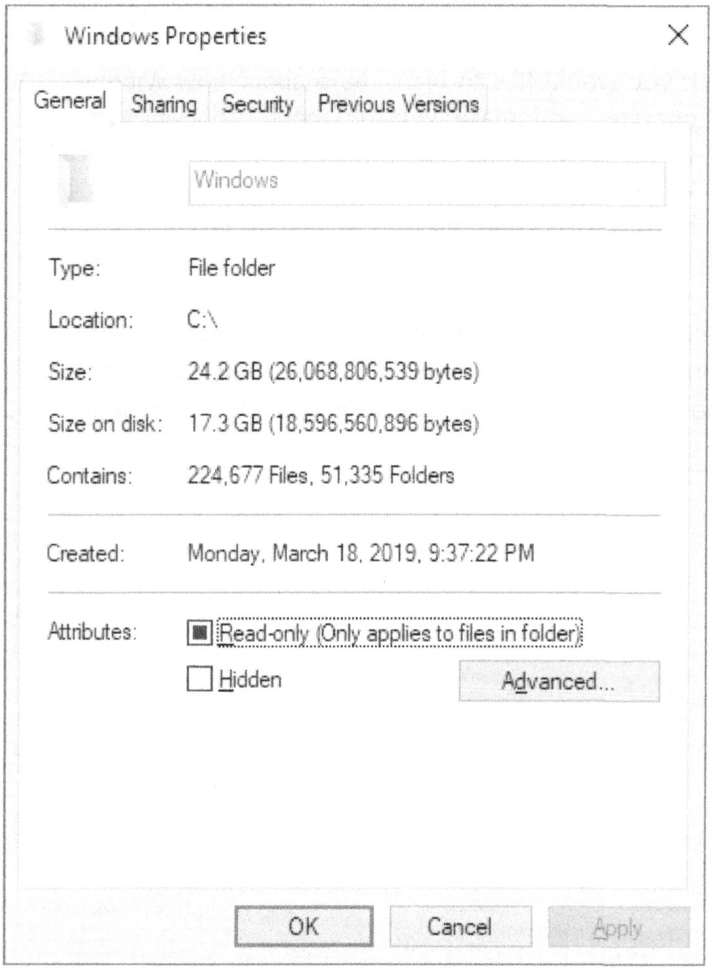

Figure 3.9

As you can see, there are many files and folders located here and for the most part, you won't need to do anything here unless you are maybe performing some type of troubleshooting or program customization. For example, let's say you are having a problem with a driver for a piece of hardware installed on your computer. It might be good to know that most of the driver files are located under *C:\Windows\System32\drivers*. Or if you want a quick way to see the fonts installed on your computer you can find them in *C:\Windows\Fonts*.

Chapter 4 – Manipulating Your Files and Folders

Now that I have covered all the educational, boring stuff, it's now time to get into the fun part of the book and actually start managing our files and folders. This is the chapter you really want to pay attention to because I will be going over the most commonly used file and folder management tasks.

Creating Files and Folders

When you buy a computer, obviously it will come with files and folders on it and when you save files from the various programs you use, they will place files on your computer as well. But there will most likely come a time when you need to create files and folders on your own and fortunately it's a very easy process.

Some reasons for manually creating files and folders might include making a folder to store files such as vacation pictures or creating a blank text file to use for taking notes. The process for creating files and folders is similar but you have more choices when it comes to creating files.

Creating Folders

Since creating folders is very straightforward, I will go over how to do this first. Just like with many things in Windows, there is more than one way to create a folder so I will go over two of the most common ways.

The way I like to create a folder is to go to the location in File Explorer where I want to create the folder. Then I simply right click on a blank area and choose *New > Folder* as seen in figure 4.1

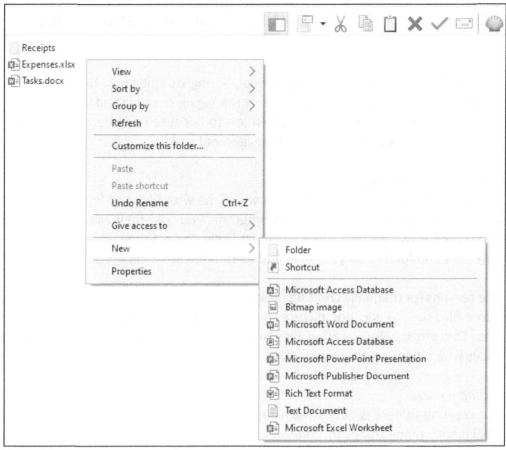

Figure 4.1

Windows will make a new folder that is named *New folder*. If you press enter on your keyboard or click out of the New folder text then the name of the folder will remain as New folder.

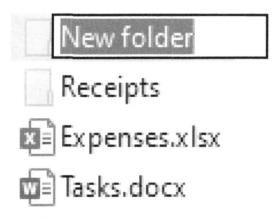

Figure 4.2

Since the text is highlighted that means you can type over it and change the name to whatever you like. If you clicked off the folder you can simply right click on it and choose *Rename* and then type in the new name for the folder. I will name my folder *Invoices*.

There are several characters that cannot be used for file or folder names in Windows. If you try to use them then you will be told that it is not allowed, and Windows won't let you include them in the name. These characters include < > : " / | \ ? *

Another way to create a new folder is to once again go to the location you want the folder to be created in and then click on the *Home* tab and then the *New folder* button and it will once again create a new folder named New folder and you can rename it just like you did before if needed.

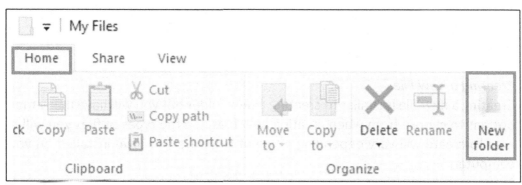

Figure 4.3

When you are working with your various software applications on your computer you will also have the option to make a new folder when performing actions such as saving a file. Figure 4.4 shows the *Save As* dialog box for Microsoft Word and you will notice that there is an option to make a new folder from here as well so you can save your file into a new folder on the spot.

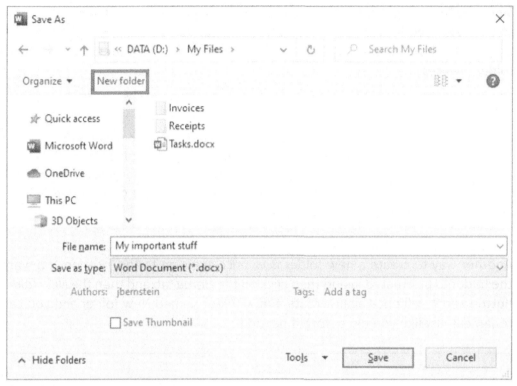

Figure 4.4

Creating a New File

Creating a new file is similar to creating a new folder but you will have many more options to choose from when creating new files and the types of files you will be able to create will vary depending on what software you have installed on your computer.

The way I like to create a new file is to navigate to the folder I want to create the file in using File Explorer and then right click in a blank area in that folder and then choose *New* and then select the type of file I want to create. As you can see in figure 4.5, I have several file types to choose from such as a bitmap image, Word document, text document and so on.

If I didn't have Microsoft Office installed on my computer I wouldn't get any of the Office file types as a choice from within the New menu. If you have different software installed than I do, then you might have some choices that I don't have shown here.

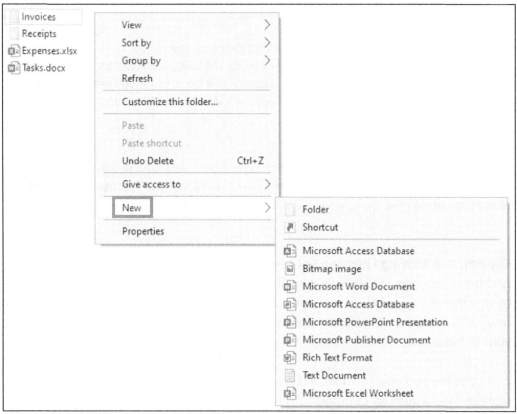

Figure 4.5

Once you select a file type it will give it a name such as *New Text Document* or New *Microsoft Bitmap Image* and you can then rename the file using the same method you used for renaming a folder. Just be sure to leave the file extension as is otherwise your computer won't know how to open the file when you try and do so after creating it.

Figure 4.6 shows another way to create a new file from the File Explorer *Home* tab. Just click on New item and you will have the same choices as seen in figure 4.5

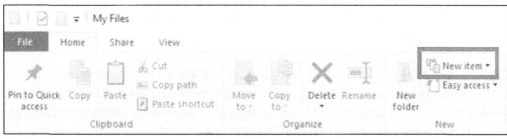

Figure 4.6

 It is possible to customize the items under the right click New menu by editing the Windows Registry. This process is beyond the scope of this book but if you want to get techy and figure it out then you can find instructions online.

Don't forget that you can easily create new files from within your software. For example, if you are in Microsoft Word you can go to the File menu and click on New to create a new document, give it a name and then save it wherever you like.

Copying and Moving Files and Folders
Just because a file or folder is stored in a certain location doesn't mean it needs to stay there. Yes, there are exceptions, such as files that are used to run Windows or your software that need to stay where they are to prevent your programs or your computer itself from not working.

It is possible to copy or move files and folders to other folders and even other storage media such as CDs, flash drives, network drives, cloud storage and so on. The main thing to keep in mind is what will happen if you copy or move a file or folder from one location to another (if anything) and whether or not you have room at the new location to store these files and folders.

There is a big difference between copying files and folders and moving them so I will now discuss each of these topics separately so you will know the difference and be able to make the right choice when it comes to both of these processes.

Copying Files and Folders
When you copy a file or folder, you are doing just that, creating a copy of an existing file or folder. This means that the original file or folder says intact in its original location and you are simply making a copy in a different location. One thing to be aware of is that you can't have two files or folders with the same name in the same location (folder).

Copying files and folders is just as easy as copying and pasting text in a document. It's just a matter of selecting what you want to copy and then pasting it where you want it to go. Once again there is more than one way to do the process so I will now go over a couple of ways to perform a copy.

Going back to File Explorer, browse to the location of the file or folder you wish to copy. Then simply right click on that file or folder and choose *Copy* or just highlight it and use the *Ctrl+C* keyboard shortcut.

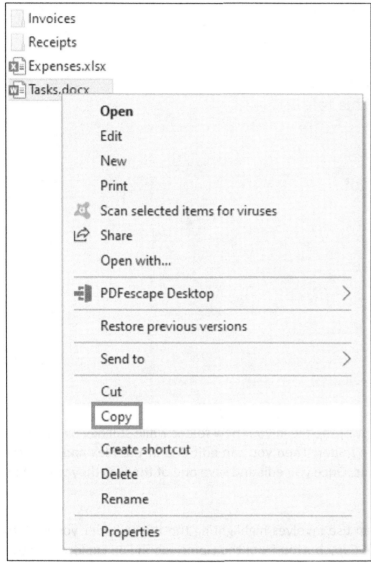

Figure 4.7

Then all you need to do is go to the folder where you want to put the file and right click in a blank spot and choose *Paste* (or the Ctrl-V shortcut). Just be careful not to choose *Paste shortcut*, because that is not the same thing, and I will be discussing shortcuts later in the chapter.

Figure 4.8

Then you will have a copy of the file in your new folder while still having the exact same copy in the source folder. Then you can edit one of the files and have the other file remain as it was. Once you edit and save one of the files they will not be exact copies anymore.

Another method you can use involves highlighting the file or folder you wish to copy and then using the *Copy* button from the Home tab in File Explorer to copy the file or folder (figure 4.9). Then you would go to where you wanted to paste the item and click on the *Paste* button from the Home tab.

Once you have the file or folder highlighted you can also use the *Copy to* button from the Home tab to choose a destination location from the dropdown list and have Windows perform the process for you.

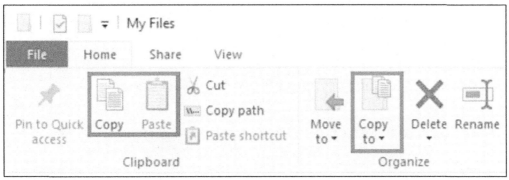

Figure 4.9

Technically it is possible to copy and paste a file or folder into the same folder, but Windows will give it a new name automatically since you can't have files with the exact same name in the same folder as I mentioned earlier.

If you paste a file into the same folder then Windows will add – *Copy* to the end of the file name as seen in figure 4.10 with the file called **Tasks.docx**.

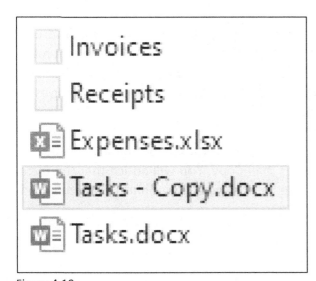

Figure 4.10

If you were to try and drag a file with the same name from one folder into another folder that contains a file with the same name then you will be prompted as to what you would like to do with that file (figure 4.11). You can either replace the file with the new one you are dragging into the folder, skip the process altogether or compare both files and decide which one you want to keep. You will also have the choice to have one of them renamed so you can then have both files in that same folder.

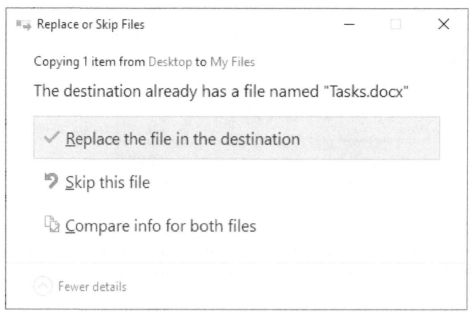

Figure 4.11

Moving Files and Folders

Moving files and folders is very similar to copying them with the main difference being that you don't end up with two copies but rather take one from one folder and move it to another folder. Technically what Windows does is copy the file or folder to the new folder and then delete the source file or folder but as far as we are concerned, it actually gets moved.

To move a file or folder simply highlight the file or folder you want to move, right click it and this time choose *Cut* rather than Copy. You will notice that the file or folder icon becomes dim as seen in the before and after graphic (left and right) in figure 4.12.

Figure 4.12

This indicates that the file has been "cut" and is ready to move or be pasted in the new location. Then you can go to the folder where you want to move the file or folder to, right click in a blank area and choose Paste just like you did for the copy process. You can also use the *Move to* button from the Home tab as seen back in figure 4.9.

Deleting Files and Folders

Deleting files and folders is pretty straightforward, and all you have to do is highlight the file or folder and click the *Delete* button on the Home tab from figure 4.9. Or you can right click a file and choose Delete or press the Delete key on your keyboard. By default, Windows will send the file or folder to the Recycle Bin rather than delete them permanently.

Depending on your Recycle Bin settings, you may or may not get a confirmation prompt asking you to confirm that you want to send the file or folder to the Recycle Bin. It will also give you details about the size of the file and the date it was modified.

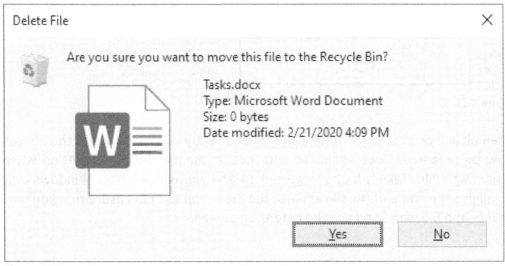

Figure 4.13

If you made a mistake and want the file back, you can use the Ctrl-Z keyboard shortcut to *undo* the action and have the file undeleted from the Recycle Bin and returned to its original location. Keep in mind that Ctrl-Z only works for the last operation performed, so if you've deleted another file since the one you wanted to be recovered, it won't work, and you will have to go into the Recycle Bin to get it back. I will be covering the Recycle Bin in more detail later in the chapter.

Renaming Files and Folders

I mentioned how you can rename a file or folder when you create a new one but it's also possible to rename them after they have been created as well as rename files and folders that you didn't create to begin with.

The process for renaming files and folders is similar to many of the other actions we have taken on our files and folders so far. All you need to do is select the file or folder you want to rename, right click on it and choose the *Rename* option. You will notice that the file or folder name will be highlighted in blue and you can either delete the name and type a new one or simply start typing and it will replace whatever text is highlighted.

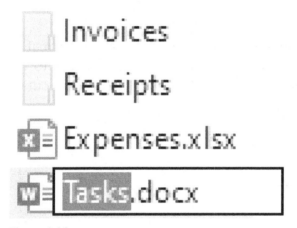

Figure 4.14

Then all you need to do is press Enter when you are done typing and the file will now be renamed. Once again, be sure not to change the file extension when renaming a file. Take a look at figure 4.14 and you will see how Windows only highlights the name of the file and not the extension to help ensure that you only change the file name and not the extension as well.

Selecting Multiple Files or Folders

Now, if you want to perform any of these file and folder operations I have been discussing to multiple files or folders, you can simply select the ones you want and then take action on them after they are selected. For example, you might want to delete, copy, move or rename a bunch of files, but don't want to have to do the process one at a time for each one. There are two ways to select multiple files depending on whether you want to select a concurrent list of files or just certain ones.

To select an entire row of files simply click on the first file in the group, hold down the *Shift* key, and then click on the last file in the group. This will highlight all the files in that particular grouping of files or folders (figure 4.15). To select a non-contiguous listing of files you can click on one file, hold down the Ctrl key, and then click on whichever files you want to highlight, and it won't highlight the entire group of files (figure 4.16).

DSC01071.JPG	DSC01098.JPG	DSC01128.JPG
DSC01072.JPG	DSC01102.JPG	DSC01129.JPG
DSC01073.JPG	DSC01103.JPG	DSC01130.JPG
DSC01074.JPG	DSC01104.JPG	DSC01131.JPG
DSC01075.JPG	DSC01105.JPG	DSC01132.JPG
DSC01076.JPG	DSC01107.JPG	DSC01133.JPG
DSC01077.JPG	DSC01108.JPG	DSC01134.JPG
DSC01078.JPG	DSC01110.JPG	DSC01135.JPG
DSC01079.JPG	DSC01111.JPG	DSC01136.JPG
DSC01080.JPG	DSC01112.JPG	DSC01137.JPG
DSC01081.JPG	DSC01114.JPG	DSC01138.JPG
DSC01082.JPG	DSC01116.JPG	DSC01139.JPG
DSC01083.JPG	DSC01117.JPG	DSC01140.JPG
DSC01086.JPG	DSC01118.JPG	DSC01141.JPG
DSC01087.JPG	DSC01119.JPG	DSC01142.JPG
DSC01088.JPG	DSC01120.JPG	DSC01143.JPG
DSC01089.JPG	DSC01121.JPG	DSC01144.JPG
DSC01090.JPG	DSC01122.JPG	DSC01145.JPG
DSC01091.JPG	DSC01123.JPG	DSC01146.JPG
DSC01092.JPG	DSC01124.JPG	DSC01147.JPG
DSC01094.JPG	DSC01125.JPG	DSC01148.JPG
DSC01095.JPG	DSC01126.JPG	DSC01149.JPG

Figure 4.15

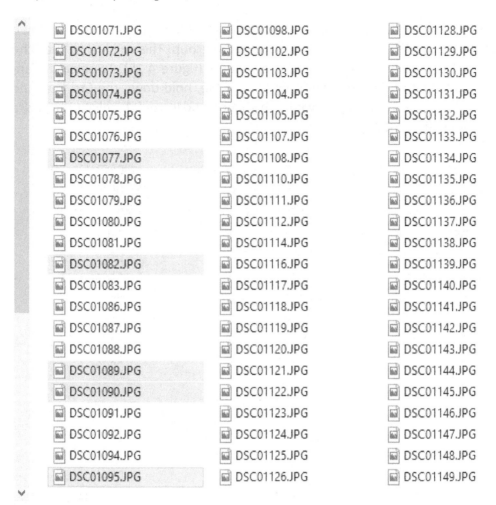

Figure 4.16

To select all the files in a folder or all of the subfolders within a folder, you can click on the *Select all* button in figure 4.17, or you can use the *Ctrl-A* keyboard shortcut. When copying, moving, renaming, and deleting files, just remember that Ctrl-Z (undo) is your friend, and if you mess something up and want to go back a step, you can use that to make your life easier.

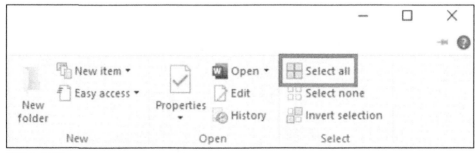

Figure 4.17

The steps to copy, move or delete multiple files or folders are pretty straightforward but if you want to rename a group of files all at once you can do that, but you are limited to how you can rename the files. Let's say you have a bunch of photos of your Hawaii trip in a folder as seen in figure 4.8.

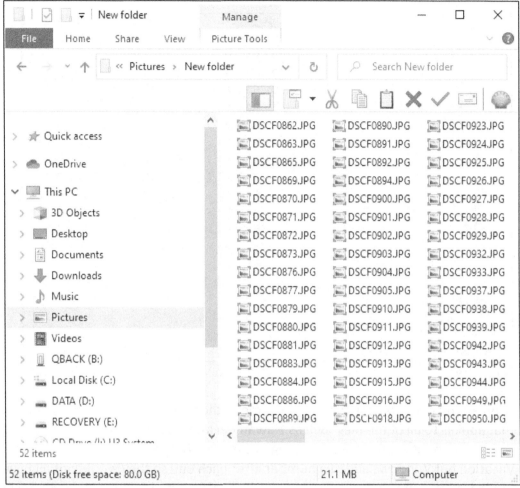

Figure 4.18

Sure you can go through and right click each one and rename them one at a time but when you have a large number of files or folders this is not too practical. Instead, you can highlight all of the photos in this folder, right click on the first one and then choose Rename. You will then notice how only the first file gets its name highlighted as seen in figure 4.19.

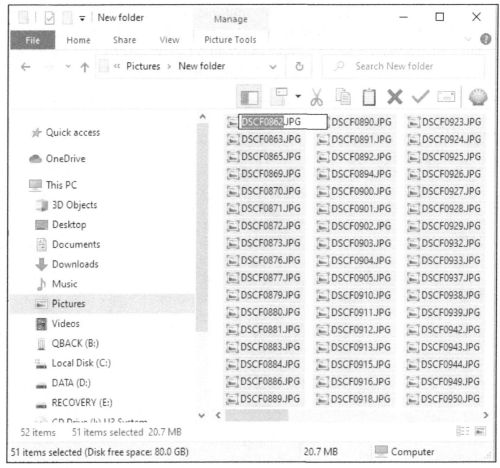

Figure 4.19

Then all you need to do is change the name of the first file to something universal that applies to all of the files such as **Hawaii Vacation** and press Enter. Figure 4.20 shows the results of the bulk renaming of the files. They all have the name Hawaii Vacation but Windows added a number after each one so they would not all have the identical name since we can't have identical files in the same folder to begin with.

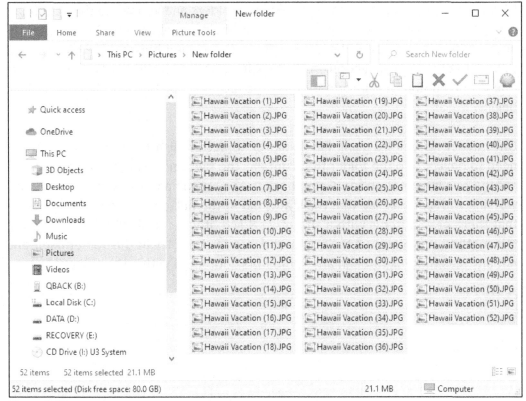

Figure 4.20

Checking File and Folder Size

When working on your computer you will come across situations where you will need to know how large a file or files are on your computer for things such as emailing them or if you are uploading them online to some cloud storage (such as Dropbox) via a slow Internet connection so you know how long it might take. Or maybe you need to transfer some files to a flash drive and want to know if you have enough room on the drive to fit them all.

If you are interested in learning about all of the popular cloud storage platforms such as Drobox, Google Drive, Amazon Drive etc. then check out my book titled **Cloud Storage Made Easy**.
https://www.amazon.com/dp/1730838359

It's very easy to find the size of your files and folders and you will find that you use a similar process to what we have been doing throughout this chapter to accomplish these goals. In fact, you might even remember that we did some of this in Chapter 2 in the section on File Explorer. Just like before, there is more than one way to obtain the information on the size of your files and folders so let's begin!

Once again we will be using File Explorer to accomplish this task. First you will need to navigate to the folder that contains the files and folders that you want to get the size information for. Going back to the Hawaii pictures that we were just working with you can see that the status bar at the bottom of File Explorer tells us that there are 52 items with a size of 21.8 MB. If you recall from Chapter 2 that this method only gives us the count and size for the files in this folder itself and not any files that might be in any subfolders contained within this folder.

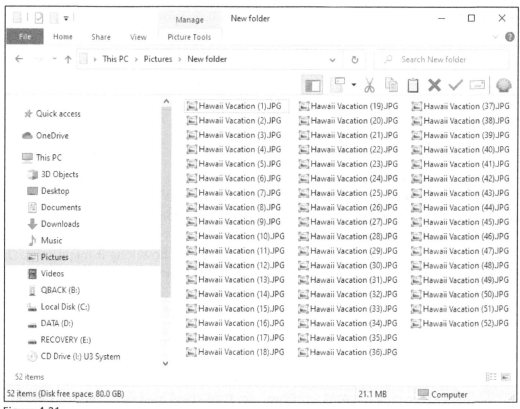

Figure 4.21

I can also highlight all of the files in the folder (Ctrl-A) and then right click on any one of them and choose Properties and I will get the same information plus some additional details as seen in figure 4.22.

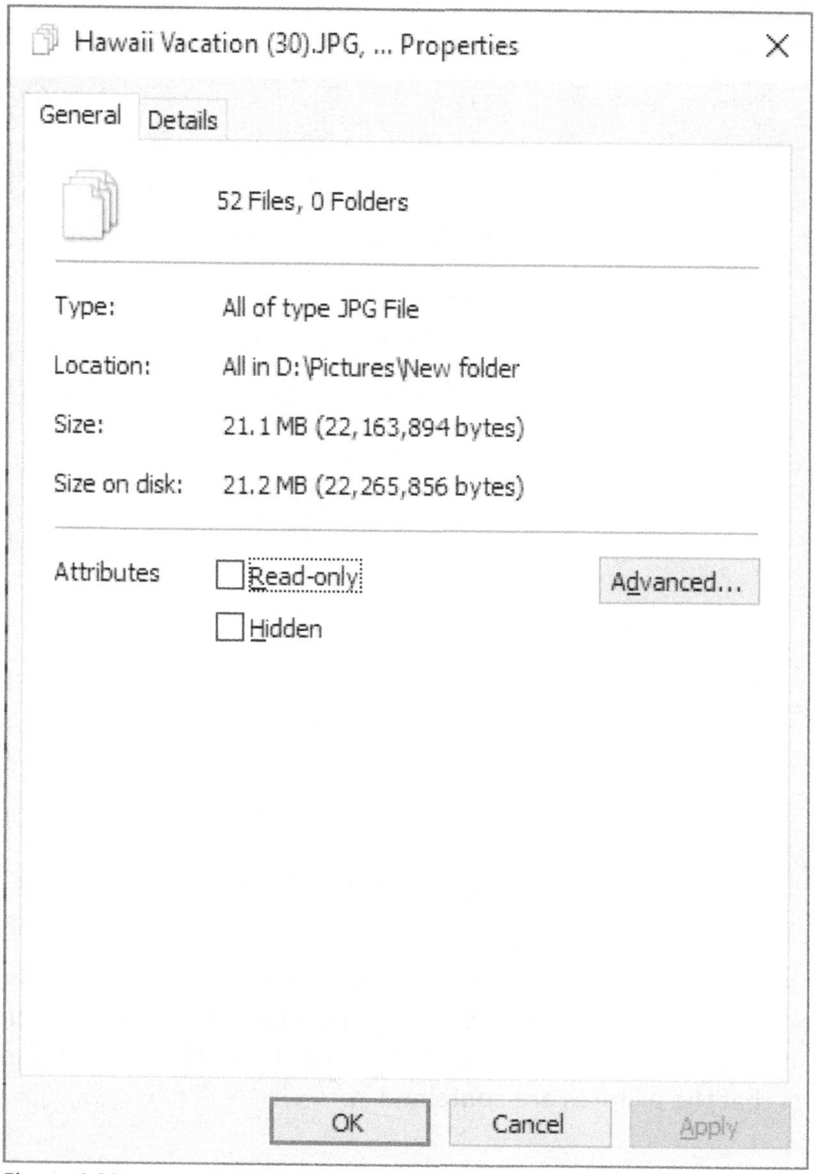

Figure 4.22

If I had all my Hawaii pictures in individual folders then the status bar would only show me the folder count and not tell me anything about the total number of files or their size (figure 4.23).

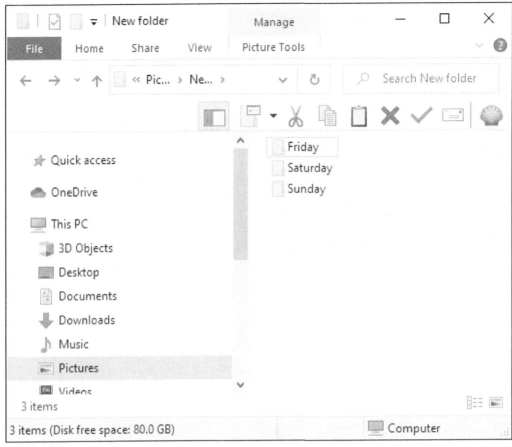

Figure 4.23

To see the size of all of the pictures in all of the folders I would need to highlight them all, right click on any of them and choose Properties once again. As you can see in figure 4.24, it shows the same 52 files with the total size of 21.1 MB but also shows the 3 folders that the pictures are contained in.

Figure 4.24

When it comes to getting an accurate file count and size value, I would use the right click, Properties method after selecting all of the files and folders you want to get the size for.

Shortcuts
You might have noticed when using your computer that you can open a program from a variety of locations such as a desktop icon, from the start menu or even from an icon on your taskbar. This doesn't mean that you have three versions of the same program installed on your computer but rather that you have three different "shortcuts" on your computer that are used to open the same program.

The concept of shortcuts for programs also applies to files and folders. You can have multiple shortcuts that "point" to the same file or folder without needing to have more than one copy of that file or folder on your computer.

I have been discussing files and folders for some time now, so you should be pretty familiar with what they are and how to manipulate them. Let's say you have an Excel workbook on your computer that is located several folders deep on your hard drive that you want easy access to. This is where a shortcut comes into play. A shortcut is simply a pointer to a file (or folder), which means it's an icon for that particular file that points to the actual location of that file. So, if you have a file called *Sales.xlsx* in a folder on your C drive under **C:\finances\business\Sales.xlsx** and want to open that file from your desktop, rather than having to navigate to c:\finances\business\Sales.xlsx each time, you would simply create a shortcut file on your desktop that points to the actual file.

There are a few different ways to create a shortcut file, but the easiest method is to locate the actual file, right click on it, and choose *Copy*. Then go to the location on your computer where you want the shortcut to that file to be (such as your desktop), then right click and choose *Paste **shortcut*** rather than choosing Paste itself as I discussed in the section on how to copy and move files. In figure 4.25, the file on the left is the original Sales.xlsx file, and the file on the right is what you will see after you paste a shortcut. Notice how it keeps the name and just adds - **Shortcut** after it. The icon also has a blue arrow indicating that it's a shortcut and not the actual file. You can rename the file to take off the shortcut label and the blue arrow will stay so you will still be able to tell it's a shortcut and not the actual file itself.

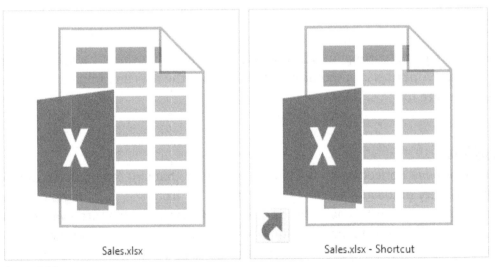

Sales.xlsx   Sales.xlsx - Shortcut

Figure 4.25

Other users on the computer can do the same process and make their own shortcuts to the same file, and you can have as many shortcuts to the same file as you like. Creating shortcuts to files is very common when the files are stored on file servers on a network where you might not know how to find the real file, or don't want to have to navigate to a networked server every time you want to open your files. Right clicking on a shortcut file and choosing *Properties* will tell you the path (or target) to the actual file if you want to know what your shortcut is pointing to. If you decide you don't want a shortcut to a file anymore, you can simply delete the shortcut and the actual file will not be affected. (Just be careful that you are deleting the shortcut and not the file itself!).

The process for creating folder shortcuts works the exact same way but once again, just make sure to choose *Paste **Shortcut*** rather than just choosing Paste, otherwise you will have a duplicate copy of the folder and ALL its contents in the location you performed the paste procedure.

You can create shortcuts to other things besides files and folders. Another way to create a shortcut is to simply right click in the location where you want to create the shortcut and choose *New > Shortcut*. You will then be prompted to type in the location (path) to the file, folder, program, website address etc. or you can click the *Browse* button and navigate to its location.

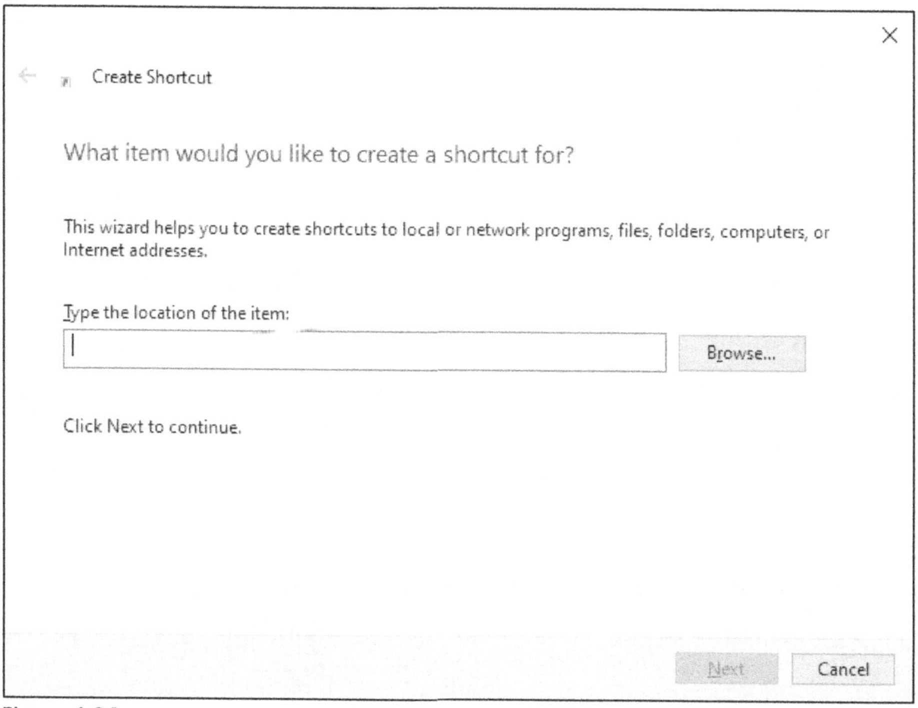

Figure 4.26

Most of the time you will want to use the Browse option rather than trying to remember the path to the item and also reduce the risk of typing it in wrong. If you already have the path handy then you can copy and paste it into the location box. When you click on Browse you will see the familiar list of drives and folders that you have on your computer and you can navigate like you normally would to find the right item that you want to create the shortcut to. You can even create a new folder and then create a shortcut to it right from here.

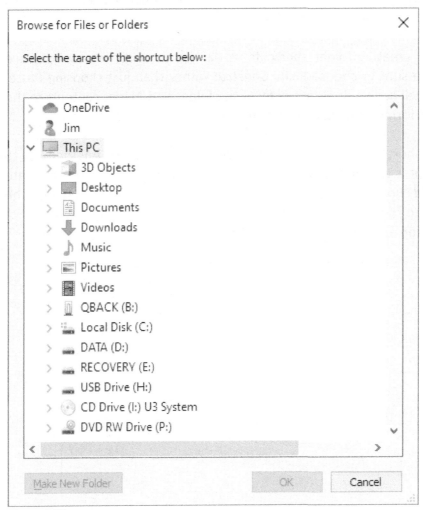

Figure 4.27

Once you choose the item you wish to create the shortcut for it will be shown in the list. In my case, I chose a folder called My Files on my D drive.

Figure 4.28

Then you can give it any name you like or keep the default which will be the name of the folder itself. I decided to give it my own custom name.

Figure 4.29

As you can see in figure 4.30, I now have a new shortcut to the folder called My Files that is named My very important files. You can tell it's a shortcut by the blue arrow next to the folder and if I were to delete this shortcut folder it would only delete the shortcut icon and not the actual folder itself.

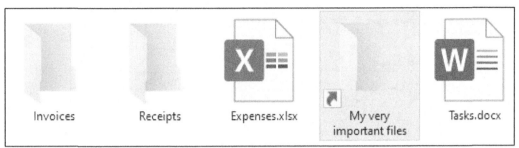

Figure 4.30

The Recycle Bin

Deleting files and folders is a common process when it comes to using your computer. There might be a time when you are done working on a document that you don't need or maybe you downloaded some pictures from your phone that didn't turn out so great and you want to get rid of them.

One thing I can guarantee is that there will be a time where you delete a file or folder and then go oops I didn't mean to do that! Thankfully when you accidentally delete a file or folder it's not the end of the world and is very easy to get back.

When you delete a file or folder, Windows will send it to the Recycle Bin rather than delete them permanently. If you made a mistake and want the file back, you can use Ctrl-Z to undo the action and have the file undeleted from the Recycle Bin and returned to its original location. Remember that Ctrl-z only works for the last operation performed, so if you've deleted another file or folder since the one you wanted to be recovered, it won't work, and you will have to go into the Recycle Bin to get it back.

If you want to see all the files you have deleted, you can open the Recycle Bin from the desktop, or, if for some reason you don't have an icon for it, you can get to it by typing **C:\$Recycle.Bin** in the File Explorer address bar, but you will need to have the *hide protected operating system files* option unchecked in the Windows Folder Options which I will be discussing in the next chapter.

Once you are in the Recycle Bin you can sort the deleted files and folder by things such as name, size, original location, date deleted, and so on (sorting files and folders will be discussed in the next chapter). If you want to recover a deleted file or folder, simply right click on it and choose *Restore*. You can also do this for multiple files and folders at a time. This will move the file back to its original location. You can also right click the file, choose Cut, and then paste it wherever you like or simply drag it out of the Recycle Bin to a different location.

If you right click the Recycle Bin and choose *Properties*, or click the Properties icon in the toolbar, you will see its location and how much hard drive space is allocated to hold recycled files.

Figure 4.31

These settings can be modified to give you more space for recycled files and folders if needed. You can also see that there is an option to bypass the Recycle

Bin and delete the files off the computer instead. This can also be accomplished manually by holding down the *Shift* key while deleting files or folders. Just know that if you do this, the files are gone for good (unless you use some type of file recovery software to get them back). Plus, there is never a guarantee that the recovery will work, and the longer you wait to recover them, the more likely the sectors the file occupies on the hard drive will get overwritten with new data.

If you run out of allocated space for the Recycle Bin then the next time you go to delete a file or folder it will tell you that it will be deleted permanently rather than sent to the Recycle Bin. Try not to use the Recycle Bin as a storage folder since it can fill up quickly.

If you do need to recover some deleted files, I recommend using a free program called Recuva by Piriform. https://www.ccleaner.com/recuva

Chapter 5 – Searching for Files and Folders

One of the most important things you need to know when it comes to file and folder management is how to find your files and folders because if you don't know where things are or even remember what they are called then you obviously won't be able to get things done!

Folder Options

Before I get into searching for files and folders I want to discuss the Windows Folder Options since the settings here will affect your search results, so it's important to have things configured correctly.

The easiest way to get to these folder options is by opening up File Explorer and then clicking on the *File* tab and then select *Options*. The Folder Options section is broken up into 3 different tabs called *General*, *View* and *Search*. We will mainly be concerned with the View and Search tabs.

Figure 5.1 shows the choices we have on the *View* tab and there are a few changes that I like to make here on every computer I work with. The first change I make is to check the radio button next to Show hidden files, folders, and drives. By doing this you will be able to access many of the Windows system folders that are normally hidden such as the *App Data* folder under the User folder for your user account which contains data for various software applications installed on your computer.

More importantly, I like to uncheck the box next to *Hide extensions for known file types* which will make Windows show the file extensions for all files rather than certain ones. In my opinion this should be disabled by default because it's nice to know what types of files you are looking at while in File Explorer.

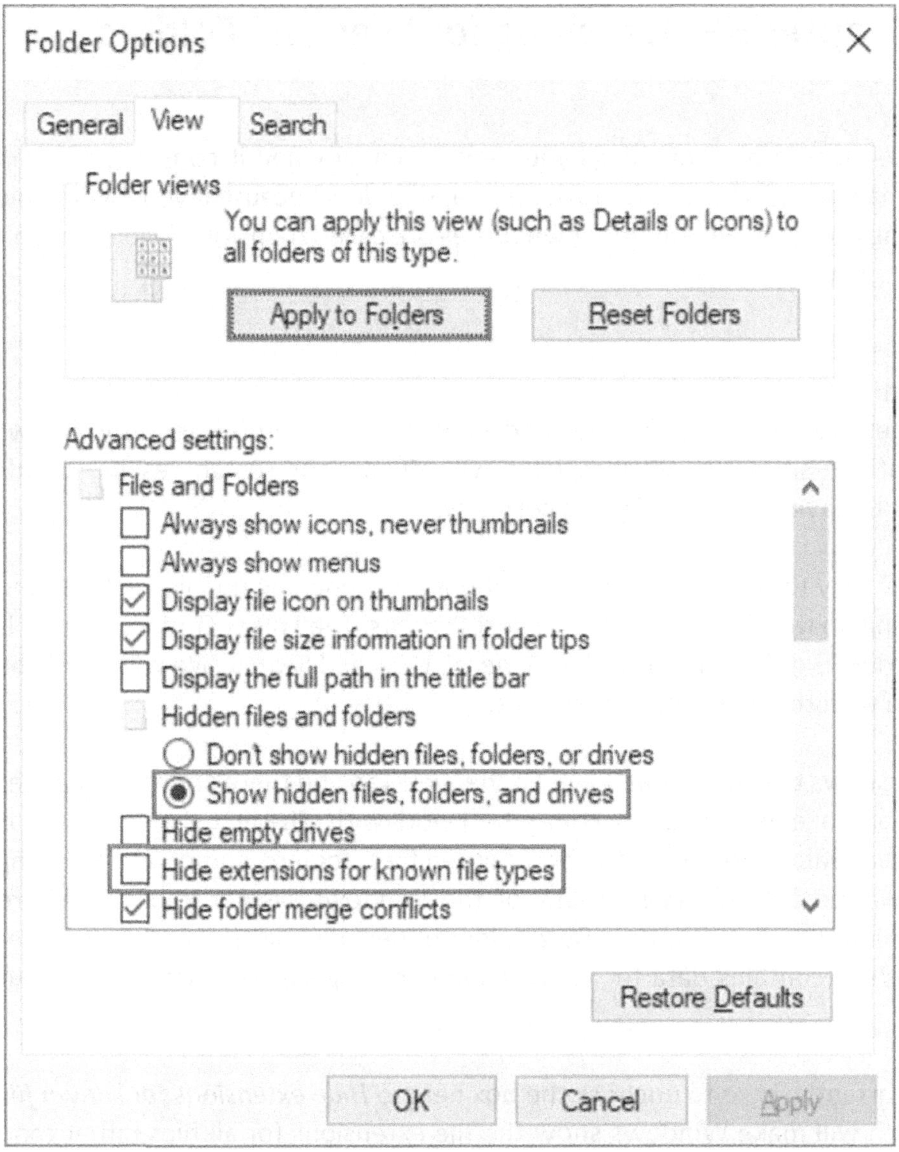

Figure 5.1

The default options on the Search tab should be fine for search purposes but I want to take a moment and describe what you are seeing on this tab. When Windows indexes your files, it means that it is that your computer creates an index of all files similar to a database index which greatly improves the speed of your searches. So if your options are different than what is shown in figure 5.2, you might want to think about changing them to match or click the *Restore Defaults* button.

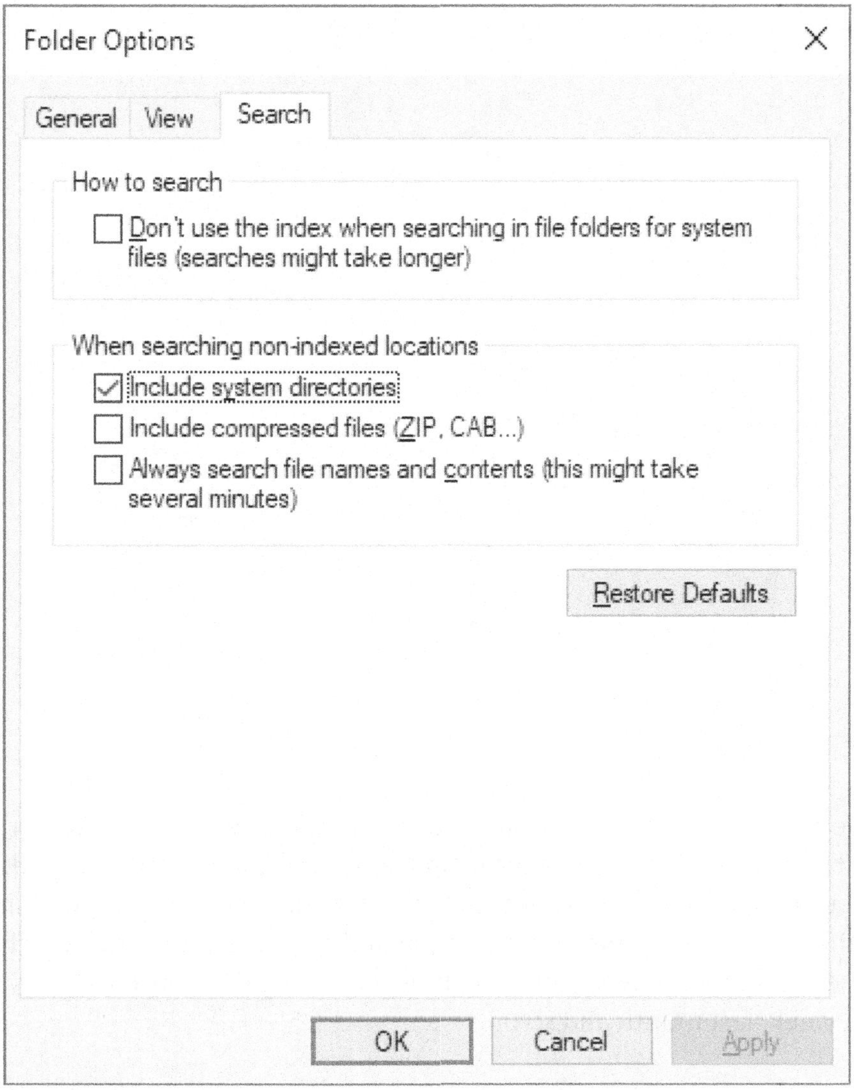

Folder Options ⊠   ✕

General View **Search**

How to search

☐ Don't use the index when searching in file folders for system files (searches might take longer)

When searching non-indexed locations

☑ Include system directories
☐ Include compressed files (ZIP, CAB...)
☐ Always search file names and contents (this might take several minutes)

Restore Defaults

OK   Cancel   Apply

Figure 5.2

Windows Search Tools

Searching for files and folders is pretty easy, and you can fine tune your searches to really narrow things down. The easiest way to do a search is to open Windows\File Explorer and navigate to the folder you want to search and then use the Windows search tools to find what you are looking for. If you don't know what folder the file (or folder) might be in, then you can search the entire PC by clicking on *This PC*. The search box is located at the upper right-hand side of the window, and once you click in the search box, the *Search* tab will become active (figure 5.3).

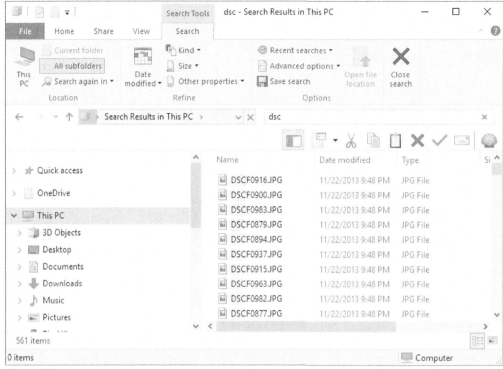

Figure 5.3

To do a simple search, type in the file or folder name you want to search for. Windows will begin searching automatically and show you the results as it finds them. You can use the options on the Search tab to fine tune your searches, such as specifying the type of file or the size of the file and so on. You can also search by date modified to narrow down your search using time periods such as today, yesterday, last week, last month and so on.

If you plan on using your custom configured search again, you can save the search by clicking on the *Save search* button. Clicking on *Recent searches* will show you the items you searched for in the past and allow you to search for them again. If you only want to search the current folder, then click on the Current folder button, otherwise leave it on *All subfolders* to search all the subfolders of the folder you are currently in.

One effective way to search for files is to use wildcards. These come in handy when you know part of the name, or at least know what type of file it is that you are looking for. For example, if you know you have a file that might have been called **Birthday2018,** or maybe **Bday2018,** but aren't sure, you can use the wildcard symbol, which is an asterisk (*), and search for ***2018** to bring up any file that has some characters and then 2018 afterward or **Bday*** to search for any file starting with Bday and having anything after it. Or, if you want to search for all the jpeg images on your computer, you can search for ***.jpg**, which will search for any file with .jpg on the end (which is the file extension for jpeg images). Keep in mind that if you are searching for a popular file type then you will most likely get more results than you really want. Figure 5.4 shows that I get 24,333 files when I search for image files that end with *jpg.

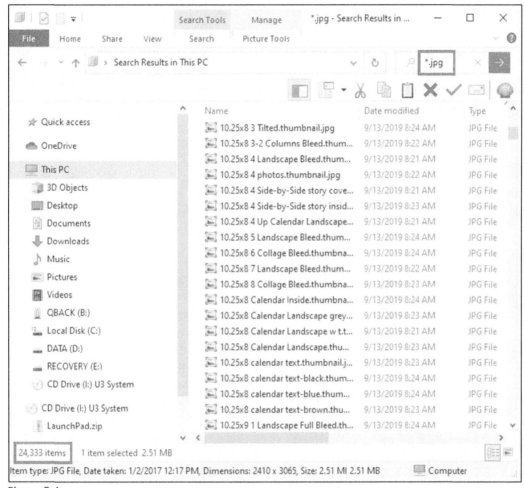

Figure 5.4

Sorting Your Files and Folders

I could have discussed this next topic earlier in the book, but I wanted to save it for the chapter on searching because you will find it very useful when trying to make sense of your search results. Going back to my last example where I have 24,333 picture files from my search results, it makes sense that I will want to sort the results to help find what I am looking for. Keep in mind that the concepts I go over here also apply to your everyday file management as well.

When you are using the File Explorer Details view you will see various attributes for your files and folders such as date modified, size, location and so on. You can sort your search results on any one of the columns that are displayed here. Also remember that you can add more columns to this list by going to the *View* tab and clicking on the *Add columns* button.

For example, if I were to click on the *Date modified* column header it would sort the files in chronological order from newest to oldest as seen in figure 5.5. Then if I were to click on the Date modified column header again it would sort them from oldest to newest.

Name	Date modified	Type	Size	Folder
IMG_20200220_104618.jpg	2/20/2020 10:46 AM	JPG File	4,427 KB	Add to Tra
IMG_20200220_104049.jpg	2/20/2020 10:40 AM	JPG File	4,892 KB	Add to Tra
IMG_20200220_103320.jpg	2/20/2020 10:33 AM	JPG File	4,512 KB	Add to Tra
IMG_20200220_103116.jpg	2/20/2020 10:31 AM	JPG File	4,440 KB	Add to Tra
IMG_20200220_102437.jpg	2/20/2020 10:24 AM	JPG File	4,298 KB	Add to Tra
IMG_20200220_102308.jpg	2/20/2020 10:23 AM	JPG File	4,860 KB	Add to Tra
IMG_20200220_101711.jpg	2/20/2020 10:17 AM	JPG File	4,486 KB	Add to Tra
IMG_20200220_101212.jpg	2/20/2020 10:12 AM	JPG File	4,573 KB	Add to Tra
IMG_20200220_101108.jpg	2/20/2020 10:11 AM	JPG File	4,901 KB	Add to Tra
IMG_20200220_100911.jpg	2/20/2020 10:09 AM	JPG File	5,124 KB	Add to Tra
IMG_20200220_100533.jpg	2/20/2020 10:05 AM	JPG File	5,453 KB	Add to Tra
IMG_20200220_100312.jpg	2/20/2020 10:03 AM	JPG File	4,839 KB	Add to Tra
IMG_20200220_095819.jpg	2/20/2020 9:58 AM	JPG File	4,034 KB	Add to Tra
IMG_20200220_095814.jpg	2/20/2020 9:58 AM	JPG File	3,380 KB	Add to Tra
IMG_20200220_095314.jpg	2/20/2020 9:53 AM	JPG File	4,798 KB	Add to Tra
IMG_20200220_095001.jpg	2/20/2020 9:50 AM	JPG File	5,054 KB	Add to Tra
IMG_20200220_094658.jpg	2/20/2020 9:46 AM	JPG File	4,805 KB	Add to Tra
IMG_20200220_094555.jpg	2/20/2020 9:45 AM	JPG File	4,895 KB	Add to Tra
IMG_20200220_094514.jpg	2/20/2020 9:45 AM	JPG File	5,015 KB	Add to Tra
IMG_20200220_094411.jpg	2/20/2020 9:44 AM	JPG File	3,742 KB	Add to Tra

Figure 5.5

You can do the same process for any of the column headers that are in use but keep in mind that if you have a large number of files that it might take a little time to update the search results.

Chapter 6 - File and Folder Permissions

If you are sharing your computer with other users then you need to have some basic knowledge about file and folder permissions to make sure that your nosy users don't go looking at each other's files. If you don't share your computer with others but do access files and folders on a network then this information will still come in handy. This chapter will cover the basics of file and folder sharing and permissions to hopefully give you a good understanding of how they work and when you should use or adjust them.

Sharing Files and Folders
Think of the concept of sharing files and folders as being similar to sharing a physical file folder and the papers inside of it. You can let some people see that you have that particular folder and you can let other people see what is inside that folder. Then to take things a step further, you can let certain people make changes to the documents that are contained in your folder.

Like I mentioned earlier in this book, your profile folder inside of the Users folder is blocked from other users unless they have administrator rights on the computer where your profile folder is stored. Once again, your profile folder contains things such as your documents, photos, music, videos and desktop files.

Any files that are not in your profile folder are fair game for others to view and even modify (with some exceptions). So if you save a document in a folder on your C drive called *Important Files* for example then other users who log into the computer will be able to see that folder and the file inside of it. So if I create this same file on my computer, right click it and choose *Properties* and then go to the *Security* tab (figure 6.1), I can see that anyone who authenticates (logs in) to this computer will be able to do almost anything to the folder and its contents by looking at what items have checkmarks next to them.

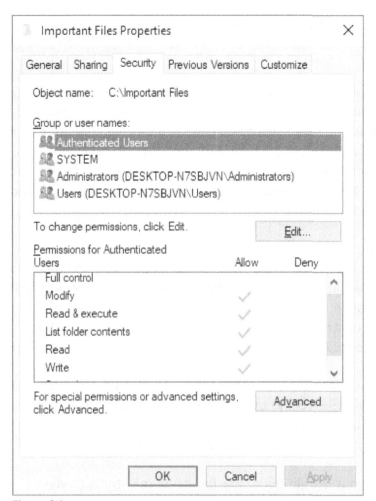

Figure 6.1

So when you are working with files and folders on a shared computer that are not stored within your user profile folders you will need to adjust these settings so that only the people you want accessing them will be able to do so. Clicking on the *Edit* button will allow you to add users or make the changes to existing user permissions that are needed to either lock down or allow access to your files and folders.

Once you add a user account then you can decide what type of access that person will get to the folder in question and check the box next to the type of access you want to give them (figure 6.2). You can only add user accounts that have already been configured on the computer. For local users on the same computer, you will be using NTFS permissions and not Share permissions. Both of these are discussed in the next section.

Permissions for Important Files   ✕

Security

Object name: C:\Important Files

Group or user names:

- 👥 Authenticated Users
- 👥 SYSTEM
- 👥 Administrators (DESKTOP-N7SBJVN\Administrators)
- 👥 Users (DESKTOP-N7SBJVN\Users)

[Add...]   [Remove]

Permissions for Authenticated Users

	Allow	Deny
Full control	☐	☐
Modify	☑	☐
Read & execute	☑	☐
List folder contents	☑	☐
Read	☑	☐

[OK]   [Cancel]   [Apply]

Figure 6.2

Be VERY CAREFUL when changing permissions on existing files and folders so you don't accidentally lock yourself out of something and never change permissions on things such as Windows system files and any program files.

Share and NTFS Permissions

Now I will discuss file and folder shares and the different types of permissions that go along with them. For files and folder sharing and permissions, once again the easiest way to begin is by right clicking on the item you want to share or view the sharing stats of, and then choose *Properties*. From there, you will be able to see the share level permissions (Sharing tab) and then Security (or NTFS) permissions.

Share permissions are what you use to have the resource be shared on the network for other users to access. Security permissions are the levels of access you can give to those users who are allowed to use the shared resources. Just keep in mind that when share and NTFS permissions are used simultaneously, the most restrictive permission will always apply. Also know that NTFS permissions apply to users who are logged on to the computer locally (and over the network), while share permissions don't apply because you are not accessing a shared resource while logged on locally to the computer that hosts that share. Here is a summary of the share and NTFS permissions available on a Windows network. These apply to workgroups and domains.

Below is a summary of the share and NTFS permissions you can assign to your resources. Figure 6.3 shows the permissions screens for each one.

Share Permissions

- **Read** - Users can view file and folder names, open files, and run programs. The *Everyone* group is assigned *Read* permissions by default.

- **Change** - Users can do everything allowed by the *Read* permission, as well as add files and subfolders, edit files, and delete subfolders and files.

- **Full Control** - Users can do everything allowed by the *Read* and *Change* permissions, as well as change permissions for NTFS files and folders only. The *Administrators* group is granted *Full Control* permission by default.

NTFS Permissions

- **Full Control** - Users can add, modify, move, and delete files and directories, as well as their associated properties. Users can also change permissions for all files and subdirectories.

- **Modify** - Users can view and modify files and their properties, including adding files to or deleting files from a directory, or file properties to or from a file.

- **Read & Execute** - Users can run executable files, including scripts, as well as open files.

- **List folder contents** - Permits viewing and listing of files and subfolders as well as executing files.

- **Read** - Users can open files and view file properties and directories.

- **Write** - Users can write to a file as well as create files and folders.

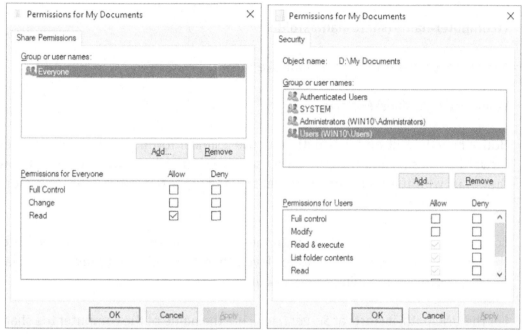

Figure 6.3

If you plan on sharing many folders with many users, you might want to come up with a game plan first and write it all down, so you are not trying to remember what you wanted to do during the process itself.

UNC Paths
If you plan on accessing shared resources on other computers on a regular basis, then you will need to know about UNC (Universal Naming Convention) paths. I have mentioned UNC paths earlier in this book but when it comes to sharing, these paths are used to navigate directly to a shared resource without having to browse to find it. They are similar to website addresses (URLs) that take you to a particular page.

For example, here is a URL (Uniform Resource Locator) for a website:

https://www.onlinecomputertips.com/support-categories/networking/298-mapping-a-network-drive

And here is a UNC path example for a shared folder that you would access over a network connection:

\\computer-name\share-name\folder

A more specific example would look like this:

\\Server1\SalesFiles\Reports

Notice how the URL and UNC path both use a similar format, except the URL uses forward slashes (/) and the UNC path uses backslashes (\). Also take note of how they start with the main server or website and work their way down to a more specific destination.

So, for the website URL, it starts with the *www.onlinecomputertips.com* website, then goes to the *support-categories* level, then the *networking* level, and then finally the page on mapping a network drive.

For the UNC path, it starts at *Server1,* which is the name of the computer the share is located on, and then goes down to the next level, which is the *SalesFiles* share itself, and finally reaches the *Reports* folder, which is inside the SalesFiles share. Then within the Reports folder you would most likely have your individual files and maybe even additional subfolders.

To use UNC paths, you can either type them into your Windows Explorer address bar or even in the Run dialog box. If you take a look at figure 6.4, you can see that I entered the UNC path in the address bar, and then Windows recognized it as one and brought up the *Computer* tab, where I have options to do things like map a network drive or add a network location.

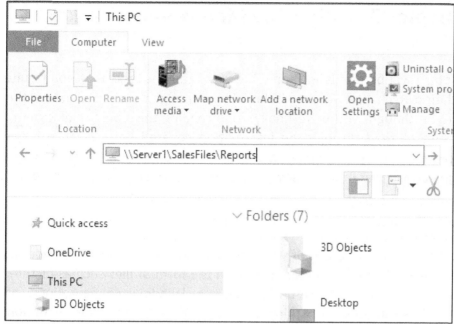

Figure 6.4

Speaking of mapping a network drive, this can be used to add a permanent (until you remove it) placeholder on your computer for that particular UNC path so you don't have to type it in each time or even remember it!

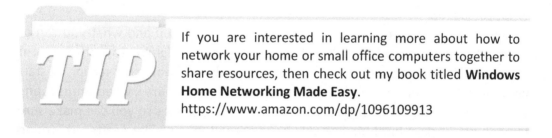

If you are interested in learning more about how to network your home or small office computers together to share resources, then check out my book titled **Windows Home Networking Made Easy**.
https://www.amazon.com/dp/1096109913

Chapter 7 – Other File Management Tasks

In this chapter I will be discussing some file management tasks that don't quite belong in their own chapter yet are still important enough to have included in this book. So if you thought you were finally done reading this book, think again! I would be sure to read through the information covered here because it will definitely come in handy at some point in your computer career. Whether it be a computer job as a career or just many years of using your computer at home.

Backing Up Data
One of the most common causes of stress and panic when it comes to computers is when you have a loss of data. Data can be in the form of files such as pictures and documents, or also in the form of software or Windows configurations and settings. Data loss can occur from things such as hardware failure, file corruption, virus and spyware attacks, and other users deleting or changing your files. You should always have a backup plan in place because you never know what will happen, and if your data is important to you, then there is no reason not to, as it can cost you hundreds or thousands of dollars to get it back if you have to use a data recovery service. In this section, I will discuss what you should be backing up, and how you can use one or more methods to do so.

What to Backup
It's up to you to determine what data is important to you and what you can or can't afford to lose. Before you decide how you are going to perform your backups, you will need to determine *what* exactly you want to backup. To start with, there are your personal files such as documents, pictures, videos, music, and so on, and you will need to know the locations of these files so you can make sure they all get backed up. Many people have these types of files scattered around their computers in various places, so you might want to consider doing some organizing before working on your backup plan. For the most part, you should have most of your files under your Users folder on your C drive under folders such as Documents, Music, Favorites, Pictures and so on, or on your Desktop, which is technically in your Users folder as well (figure 7.1).

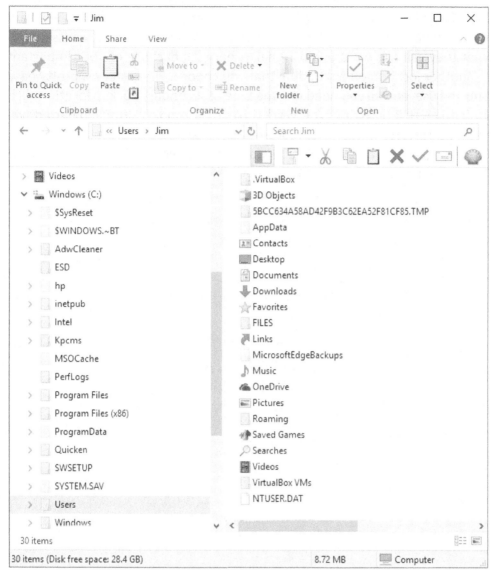

Figure 7.1

You also have software and Windows backups to consider. For the most part, you can't really back up your software, because if your computer dies and you need to get a new one or reinstall Windows, then you will have to reinstall the software as well. But sometimes there are specific configurations that have been applied to software that can be exported and backed up so they can be imported back into the new installation of the software. As for Windows itself, you can back it up so it can be recovered in case of failure, or you can back up the whole computer with the software as an image that can be restored back to the point in time when the backup took place.

Windows Backup is built into the operating system, but how it works will vary depending on your version of Windows. For example, Windows 10 wants you to use what they call *File History* which makes periodic backups of your important files to another location on a schedule that you choose. File History is pretty easy to set up and use, and all you need is some type of secondary backup location such as a flash drive, USB hard drive, network drive, or secondary attached hard drive. To open File History, navigate to *Control Panel, Security and Maintenance (or System and Security)*, and then *File History* or just type in file history in your run\Cortana search box (figure 7.2).

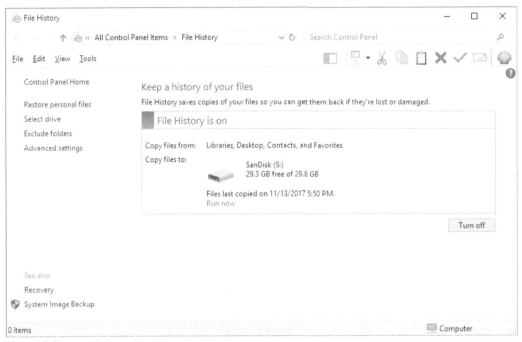

Figure 7.2

Then there is the older *Backup and Restore* feature for Windows 7 that will also work on Windows 10 (as of this writing). This type of backup will let you choose what drive to backup (if you have more than one), and where to back it up to, such as a network location. Once you go through the wizard and choose a drive to backup, you can then decide what files you want to backup, or let Windows choose for you. Choosing this option will have Windows backup the default Windows folders and create a system image that can be used to restore your computer if needed. If you pick the option to choose your own files, you will be given a chance to make a system image as well. There is also an option to change the backup schedule to suit your needs. As for the backup location, you should choose a drive that is different from the one that is being backed up.

Once you have a successful backup you can go into Backup and Restore and restore your data from the backup or run a recovery of the system image that was created during the backup (figure 7.3). There are also other options such as managing the space used by the backups where you can delete older backups to free up disk space. You can also change the backup schedule settings from here. You can access Backup and Restore from the same place as File History.

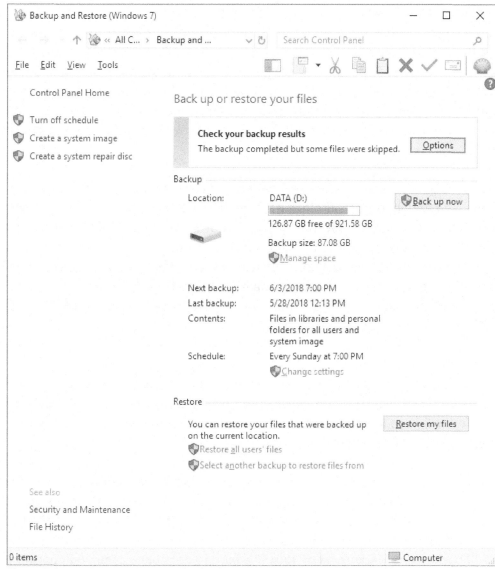

Figure 7.3

Under the *Restore* section, there are options to restore your files, and from here you can browse the backup to recover individual files or folders from the backup itself. If you have multiple backups, you can click on "Select another backup" to restore files from another date. To do an image restore you would boot with your Windows DVD or system image boot disk that you created from the Windows backup process and restore the image. This will overwrite the current files and settings with the ones from the backup, so be careful before doing so.

How Often to Backup

Now that you know what you want to backup, the next question is how often *should* you backup? The answer to that depends on how often your files change, and how current you want your backup to be. Since most backups are scheduled rather than done manually, you will need to decide at what interval you want the backup to occur, as well as the day(s) and time. If you are always editing documents or copying pictures from your camera or smartphone to your computer, then you might want to have backups occur more frequently than someone who just uses their computer mainly to browse the Internet and check email.

For the average home computer user, backing up your computer once a week will probably be enough, especially since each backup will take up room on whatever drive you decide to use for backups. If you do not want to have multiple backups but rather one backup that keeps getting overwritten, that will be an option depending on what backup software you use or if you decide to back up your files manually. Most businesses run backups daily off hours to make sure they have the most current data backed up at all times, and also keep backups for multiple days, weeks, months, and even years.

Backup Types

Not all backups are created equally when it comes to the type of backup method being used. In fact, backup strategies can be pretty complex, but for the sake of this book, I will keep it simple and tell you what you need to know to successfully backup your home or small business to keep your data safe.

When you back up your files the first time you do what is called a *full backup*. This method will back up all the files and folders you specify whether they are brand new or five years old. A full backup is used for the very first backup no matter what type of backup you are using. If you have an existing backup in place, you can still do a full backup and back up all of your files and folders once again. Full backups can overwrite existing full backups or be saved as a separate full backup with the date and time of the backup.

Next, we have what is called *incremental backups*. These types of backups only backup the files and folders that have been changed or added since the last backup. So, let's say you have 300 files in your last backup, and then 25 of them were modified or changed and 5 new files were added since that backup was run. The next incremental backup will only backup those 25 changed files plus the 5 new ones. This saves backup space because it doesn't back up files that have not been changed since there is no need to do so. But on the downside, if you needed to do a full recovery, for example, if your computer died, then you would need to restore the last full backup, *plus* every incremental backup that was run since that full backup. This can get out of control fast, and that is why full backups are run periodically so that you don't have too many incremental backups to restore since you only need to restore the incremental backups that were run since the last full backup.

Finally, we have *differential backups,* which contain all files and folders that have been changed since the last full backup, or in other words, the differences since the last full backup. So, every time this type of backup runs it will copy any files and folders that have been changed, modified, or added. For example, let's say you run a full backup on Saturday with 300 files. On Monday you modify 10 files and add 5 new files. The differential backup will copy only 15 files for the new backup. Then on Tuesday you modify 3 files and add 2 new files. Then the differential backup will copy 20 files over because it copies the 15 files from Monday and the 5 files from Tuesday. This type of backup can start to take up space quickly depending on how often you run it. The benefit of a differential backup is that you only need to restore the last full backup and the last differential backup when doing a full recovery because each differential backup has all of the files that have been changed or added since the last full backup.

Backup Hardware
The purpose of a backup is to protect your data in case of hardware failure, file corruption, or even theft, so it doesn't make sense to back up your data on the same computer as where the data itself is being stored. If you have your backups stored on your C drive, for example, and that hard drive dies, then your backup dies along with it.

If you plan on taking your backups seriously, then you need to come up with a plan to keep the backups themselves safe from harm. This means storing them on some other device or media separate from your computer, and there are several options for doing so.

- **USB Flash Drive** – This is a cheap and easy option because USB flash drives are inexpensive and easy to store somewhere safe. If you choose this option, try to rotate two flash drives in case one of them gets lost or goes bad. The downside to using a flash drive is they don't have a lot of storage capacity, so if you have a lot of files they might not all fit.

- **USB Hard Drive** – This works in a similar fashion to flash drives except you can get a lot more storage capacity, and hard drives tend to be more durable than flash drives and less likely to get lost. If you plan on having multiple backup copies from different dates, then you will need the capacity of this type of hard drive.

- **CD\DVD** – This backup method is not used too often but is a valid choice if you only plan to do full backups once in a while. CDs only hold 700MB of data and DVDs 4.4GB of data, so if you have more than that, then you are looking at using multiple disks, which might not be practical. Plus, CDs and DVDs can only be used once (unless you happen to have the rewritable type).

- **Network Location** – If you have other computers on your network, then you can backup your data to a shared drive\folder on one of the other computers (assuming you have the permissions on the other computer to do so). Just make sure that the backup location on the remote computer is secure if you are worried about other people seeing your data.

- **Tape** – Backup tapes have been used for years in the business world because they are relatively cheap and can hold a lot of data. The downside is that they are slow and require a specific tape drive to be connected to your computer to hold the backup tapes. This is not really an option for home users because it's overkill and too expensive compared to the other, more simple methods.

- **Network Storage** – In the enterprise world of backups, you can use networked attached storage to hold your backups because hard drives are cheap, depending on the type, and they have a large storage capacity. There are some small home network storage devices you can buy that are similar in the way they work but have much less storage that is most likely slower as well.

- **Cloud** – Cloud backups will be discussed later in this chapter.

Backup Software

Unless you want to manually do full backups each time you want to backup your data, you will need to run some sort of backup software to automate the process. This type of software is specifically designed to run various types of backups of your computer based on the type of backup you want to run. The cost of this software varies quite a bit based on how you are using it, and if it's for home or enterprise business use.

To backup your computer at home, I suggest starting with Windows backup or File History for Windows 10 and see how it works for you. If you need some additional features, then you can search online for some more robust backup software. You should be able to get a free trial in most cases, then you can decide if you want to buy the software or not after that.

Backup vs. Synchronization

Another way to keep your data safe is to synchronize it with another device so that you have identical copies at the source (your computer) and destination (backup device). This is different from backing up data because backups consist of the state of the files at the time of the backup, while synchronization updates the files on the destination or sometimes even the source in either real time or as scheduled by you.

Let's say on your computer you have 200 documents and you copy them to a removable hard drive so that the files on both locations are identical. Then on your computer, you make changes to 10 of them and now your computer has newer versions of those 10 documents. Your removable hard drive still has the old versions of those 10 files. If you were to synchronize the computer and removable drive, then it would copy the 10 updated files to the removable drive and overwrite the copies there, making things identical again. If you deleted a file on your computer and synchronized again, then it would delete the matching file on the removable drive to make things match once again.

Two-way synchronization is where the changes can go both ways. So, if you deleted a file on the removable drive, then it would delete that matching file on your computer when the synchronization ran again. Two-way synchronization would be more commonly used in a situation where you have two locations for the same files for redundancy or performance reasons such as matching file servers at two different sites. In this case, you want the files to be the same on each server, and when changes are made to a file on one server those changes would be synchronized to the other server.

For the most part, one-way synchronization is what you would use at home, and the direction of the synchronization would be to the removable drive or whatever backup device you are using. There are software packages out there that can do this for you, and I have had great success with one called *AllwaySync*. It is free to use unless you have too much data to sync, and then they will make you buy the professional version, but it only costs around $30.

Offsite\Cloud Backup

At some point you must have heard someone talking about "the cloud" and either wondered what they meant or maybe didn't care what they meant. But if you want to be up to date with your technology terminology and be "cool", then you should know a little about how it works.

When people talk about the cloud they are referring to servers, software, storage, and so on that is located at a remote site somewhere in the world and is accessible over the Internet. Many companies run their servers in the cloud, so they don't have to buy expensive hardware to use onsite. The same goes for licensing software where you buy a certain amount of copies that can be used by anyone with access to your account.

As for cloud backup, what you are doing is backing up your data to a server or storage device at a remote location over the Internet using whatever backup method you like (assuming its available to you). In this case, you are usually charged based on how much storage you need to use for your backups. There will be a software client that runs on your computer and backs up your data to this remote server or storage. Then, on their end, they will back it up again to make sure that they don't lose any of your data. The only downside is that your data is on some server that you most likely will never know the location of, and if the Internet is down at your location, your backup will not run, nor will you be able to recover files from your backup.

Reducing Picture File Sizes

Pictures are one of the most commonly sent email attachments, and with a good camera or smartphone, your pictures can get quite large. Common sizes for pictures these days are 6-8MB *each*, so you can see how it would be hard to send a bunch of pictures in one email. If these are just pictures that people will be viewing on their computer and not something that you are sending out for artwork or printing purposes, then you should consider shrinking them down to make the file size smaller. This usually involves using some type of photo editing software, but there is a great (and free) utility called *Image Resizer for Windows* that you can download and use to resize pictures one at a time or in bulk to make them smaller while still keeping the image quality. Once you install the software you will have a new choice called *Resize pictures* when right clicking on a photo file. Then you will be able to choose the amount of reduction that will be made to the file.

You can experiment with the different sizes, but I find that the *Large* choice usually works the best when it comes to reducing the file size adequately while still keeping the image dimensions and acceptable size. The one thing you need to be aware of is the checkbox for *Resize the original pictures (don't create copies)* because if this box is checked, the program will resize the pictures and replace the originals and you will be stuck with the size you chose and won't be able to go back to the original size. If it's not checked then it will make a resized copy of the photo in the same folder while leaving the original as is.

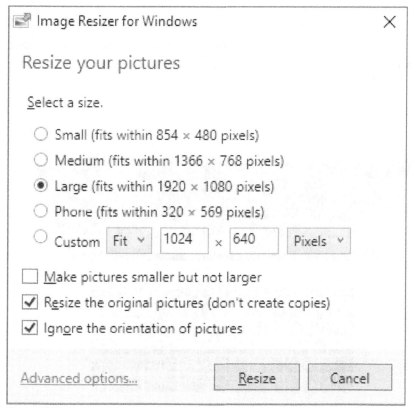

Figure 7.4

You can use this program on multiple photos at the same time by highlighting the ones you want to change and then right clicking on any one of them and go through the same process I just discussed.

Another way to include pictures in an email is to paste a copy into the body of the email rather than attach it. Just copy a picture from the source such as a website and then paste it into the email as if it were text.

Copying Files (Photos) From Your Smartphone to Your Computer

If and when you do decide that you want to transfer pictures and videos from your phone to your computer, it's a pretty easy process to do. Just keep in mind that you can either COPY pictures from your phone to your computer, or you can MOVE them. Copying them won't free up any space from your phone but moving them will.

The first step in the process is to connect the USB cable that came with your phone to the normal charging port on your phone, and then to a free USB port on your computer.

Figure 7.8

The next step involves telling your phone that you want to use the connection to your computer to transfer files. For Android phones, this is usually done by pulling down from the notification area, tapping on the USB section (figure 7.8) to open up the connection options, and choosing the appropriate action (figure 7.9).

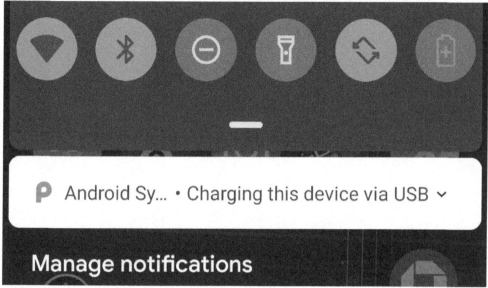

Figure 7.9

Notice in figure 7.9 that I chose the *File Transfer* option because I want to transfer files from my phone to my computer. You may see options with slightly different names such as *photo transfer,* for example.

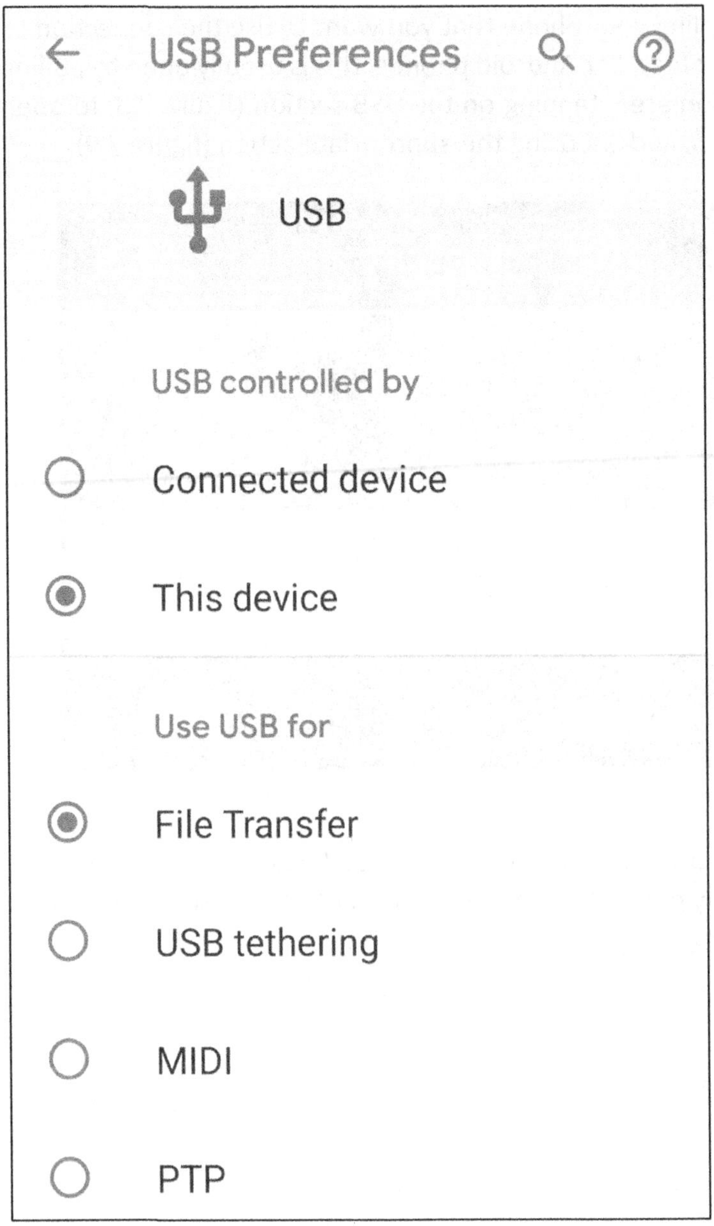

Figure 7.9

iPhones will typically pop up a message asking if you want to trust this computer, and you have to confirm before it will let you access the phone's storage from your computer.

Figure 7.10

Then on your computer you should see your phone appear. Then you can double click on its internal storage to see the files and folders contained on your phone. Figure 7.11 shows what happens when I connect my Android smartphone to my computer and tell it to use the connection for file transfers. Notice how it shows the amount of storage that is being used on my phone.

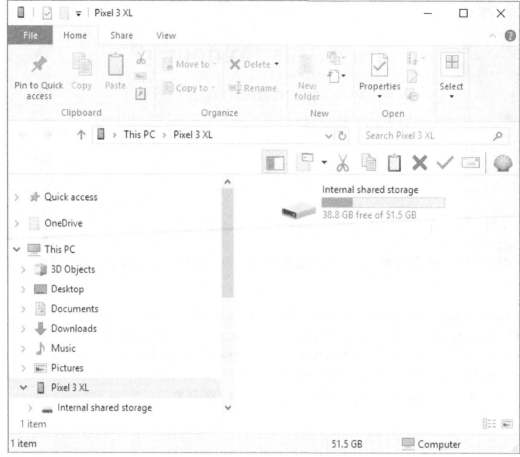

Figure 7.11

To get to my pictures I will want to find a folder named DCIM, and when I find that, I want to double click it to open it up.

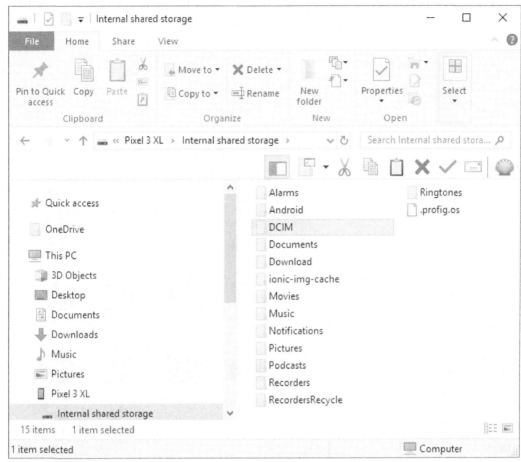

Figure 7.12

Within that folder you may see your pictures, or you might have another folder called *Camera* that you will need to open up. Once you are here, you can drag and drop the pictures from your phone to your computer and then delete them off of your phone after you confirm that they have been copied over. You can delete them using the phone, or you can delete them right from this DCIM folder that you opened up on your computer.

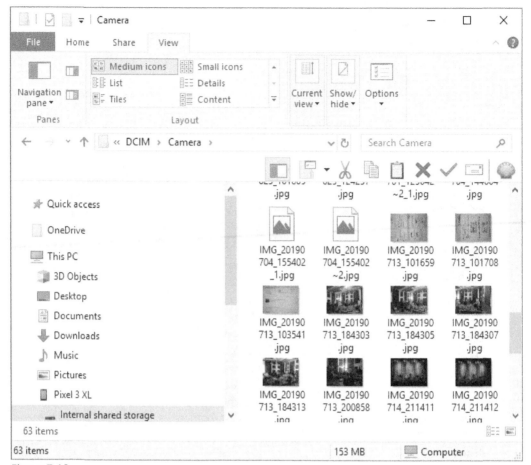

Figure 7.13

Checking Hard Drive Space Usage

I'm sure you know by now that your files and folders take up space on your hard drive or whatever location you store them at. You probably also know that storage space is not unlimited and eventually you will run out of room if you keep adding more and more files to your computer without freeing up any space by removing programs or doing other things such as uninstalling unneeded software etc.

The process to check your used and available drive space (capacity) is fairly simple and works the same way for most of the types of storage devices you might use. If you only have one hard drive then it's even easier but you can also apply this process to devices such as external hard drives, flash drives, CD\DVDs and so on.

The first step in the process is to find the drive or device you want to check the space usage for in File Explorer. Then right click on that drive or device and choose *Properties*. You will then be shown the used space, free (available) space and total space (capacity). You will also be shown what type of device it is and the file system that is being used on the drive. Figure 7.14 shows that it is a local disk and that it is formatted using the *NTFS* filesystem. Figure 7.15 shows the properties for a USB flash drive formatted with the *FAT32* filesystem.

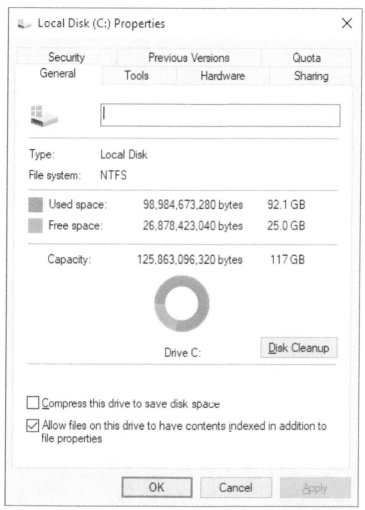

Figure 7.14

For most kinds of drives, you can change their name to something more descriptive if you like. In figure 7.15 you can see that this flash drive is named SANDISK, but I can rename it to something more descriptive if I like. Then that name will show up in your File Explorer as seen in figure 7.16.

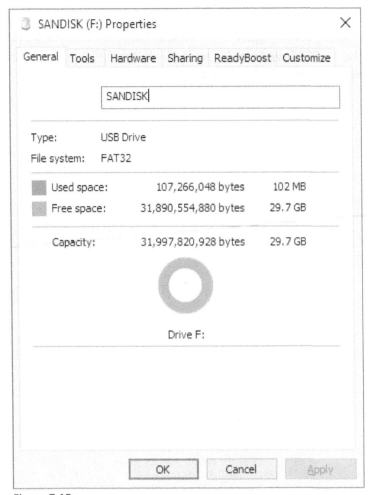

Figure 7.15

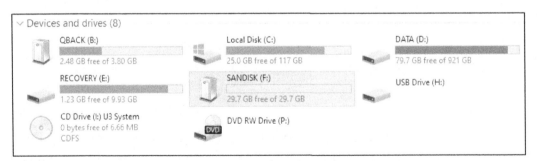

Figure 7.16

Freeing up Hard Drive Space

Now that you know how to check your hard drive space you might notice that you are running low on free space like I am on my DATA (D:) drive as seen in figure 7.16. Even though the drive is about 90% full it still shows 79 GB of space which is actually quite a bit of room, so you need to keep that in mind when looking at overall drive usage.

There are several ways to free up hard drive space on your computer and how you do this will depend on what drive you are trying to regain your space on. If it's a secondary hard drive, flash drive or external drive then you will need to delete files to recover used space. If you need to keep everything on that drive you can move these files to another drive that has more space.

You might have heard of file compression where you can compress or shrink your files, so they take up less room on the drive. I am not a fan of this because every time you access a compressed file, it needs to be uncompressed and then recompressed when you are done with it which slows things down a bit.

When it comes to freeing up space on your Windows\system drive (C:), you have a few more options. You can remove unwanted files and folders just like you can with other drives, or you can do things such as uninstall unneeded software and perform cleanup procedures on your drive that will get rid of temporary files placed on the drive by Windows and other software.

You never want to let your Windows drive run low on free hard drive space because it will cause issues such as poor performance and crashing when your computer doesn't have the space it needs to work.

There are several ways to remove temporary files and free up hard drive space so it's up to you to find the method that works best for you. There are many third party software applications that do a great job such as **Piriform CCleaner** which is a free download (https://www.ccleaner.com/).

You can also use the built in Windows drive cleanup that can be found in the Windows 10 Settings app on your computer from the *System* section and then *Storage* area (figure 7.17). Once you are there you will see the status of your C: drive and it will show you what types of items are taking up what space on your hard drive. Clicking on *Show more categories* will expand this list giving you a more in depth view of what is using your disk space.

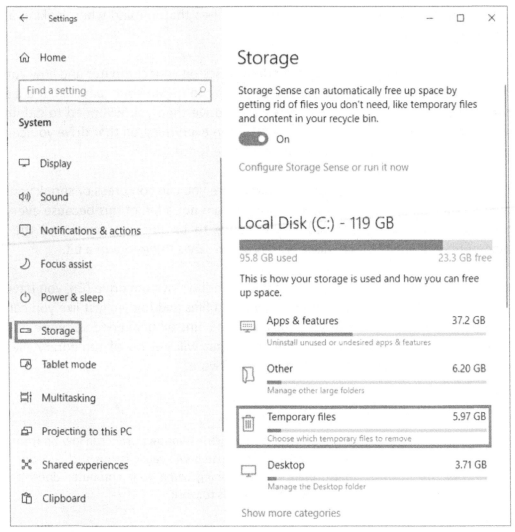

Figure 7.17

If you click on the section labeled *Temporary files* you will be shown all the different types of temporary files that are taking up space on your hard drive and be given the opportunity to remove them. As you can see from figure 7.18 that there are a lot of different categories for these files.

←   Settings   —   □   ✕

⌂   Temporary files

Some temporary files are needed by apps. Below is a list of files you can remove now.

[Remove files]   Total selected: 4.30 GB

Recycle Bin   5.11 GB
☐ The Recycle Bin contains files you have deleted from your computer. These files are not permanently removed until you empty the Recycle Bin.

Windows Update Cleanup   3.54 GB
☑ Windows keeps copies of all installed updates from Windows Update, even after installing newer versions of updates. Windows Update cleanup deletes or compresses older versions of updates that are no longer needed and taking up space. (You might need to restart your computer.)

Thumbnails   681 MB
☑ Windows keeps a copy of all of your picture, video, and document thumbnails so they can be displayed quickly when you open a folder. If you delete these thumbnails, they will be automatically recreated as needed.

Temporary files   87.6 MB
☑ Apps can store temporary information in specific folders. These can be cleaned up manually if the app does not do it automatically.

Delivery Optimization Files   14.2 MB
☐ Delivery Optimization files are files that were previously downloaded to your computer and can be deleted if currently unused by the Delivery Optimization service.

Windows error reports and feedback diagnostics   1.51 MB
☑ Diagnostics files generated from Windows errors and user feedback.

Windows upgrade log files   516 KB
☑ Windows upgrade log files contain information that can help identify and troubleshoot problems that occur during Windows installation, upgrade, or servicing. Deleting these files can make it difficult to troubleshoot installation issues.

DirectX Shader Cache   401 KB
☑ Clean up files created by the graphics system which can speed up application load time and improve responsiveness. They will be re-generated as needed.

Temporary Internet Files   94.0 KB
☑ The Temporary Internet Files folder contains webpages stored on your hard disk for quick viewing. Your personalized settings for webpages will be left intact.

Temporary Windows installation files   24.0 KB
☐ Installation files used by Windows setup. These files are left over from the installation process and can be safely deleted.

Downloads   1.84 KB
☐ Warning: These are files in your personal Downloads folder. Select this if you'd like to delete everything. This does not respect your Storage Sense configuration.

Figure 7.18

To remove these files all you need to do is check the box next to the items you wish to remove. Just make sure you know what you are doing so you don't delete any files you really needed such as the files in your Recycle Bin.

When you are ready to go simply click on the button labeled *Remove files* and Windows will do the rest. This process may take some time depending on what items you have selected and how many files need to be removed. Then you can go back and check the properties of your drive and see how much space you got back.

The Details Tab from a File's Properties
Speaking of properties, there is one more property related item I would like to discuss in this book and that is the Details tab. When you right click on a file and choose Properties you will notice that there is a tab called Details. This tab will contain various information about that file and this information will vary depending on what type of file you are looking at.

The left side of figure 7.19 shows the Details tab for a Microsoft Word document and you will see that there is a variety of information here such as the author, date created, editing time, word count and so on. You can see how this information could come in handy if you knew where to find it.

The right side of figure 7.19 shows the Details tab for a music MP3 file and here you can see things such as the song title, artist name, album year, song duration and so on. You can click on most of these fields and add or edit the information here to customize your files. Many people like to do this with MP3 files, so the band information shows up correctly on the screen when playing MPS files.

So if you are bored you can play around with different types of files and check the information that is provided in the Details tab and maybe learn something you didn't know about your files!

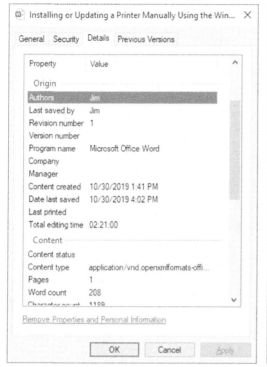

Figure 7.19

Quick Access Folder

If you are like most people, you like it when you have a shortcut you can use to get something done more quickly or find what you are looking for without too much extra effort. Thankfully Windows provides such a feature when it comes to your frequently accessed folders.

The Quick access folder is something you can use from File Explorer to access folders that you use all the time without having to go looking for them or create a shortcut on your desktop or somewhere else. By default, Windows will tend to add folders that it notices you use often to your Quick access area, but you can easily add your own folders and even disable the ability for Windows to add folders on its own.

Figure 7.20 shows an example of the Quick access area with four folders underneath it. You can see that there are push pin icons to the right of each folder indicating that they have been manually added to this area. Having these folders here allows an easy way to access them right when you open File Explorer. Think of this as being similar to favorites or bookmarks that you use with your web browser.

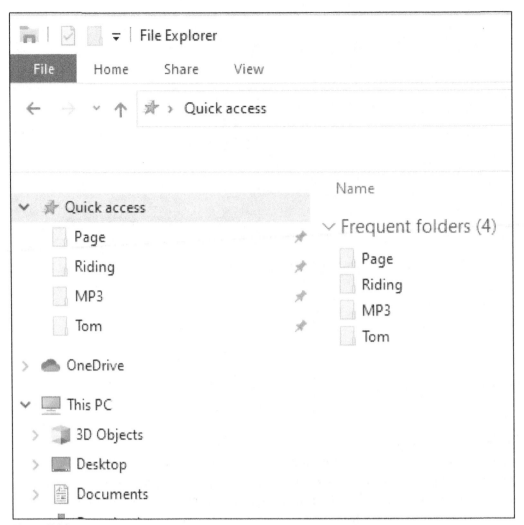

Figure 7.20

To add additional folders to this area simply locate the folder, right click on it and choose *Pin to Quick access* and it will then be added to the list. To remove a folder simply right click on it and choose *Unpin from Quick access*. You can even drag the folders around to rearrange their order. Just be careful not to drag one folder into another otherwise it will copy all of the files from one to the other.

If you want to prevent Windows from adding its own files and folders to the Quick access list then all you need to do is go back to the Windows Folder Options that were discussed in Chapter 5 and uncheck the boxes for *Show recently used files in Quick access* and *Show frequently used folders in Quick access* from the *General* tab.

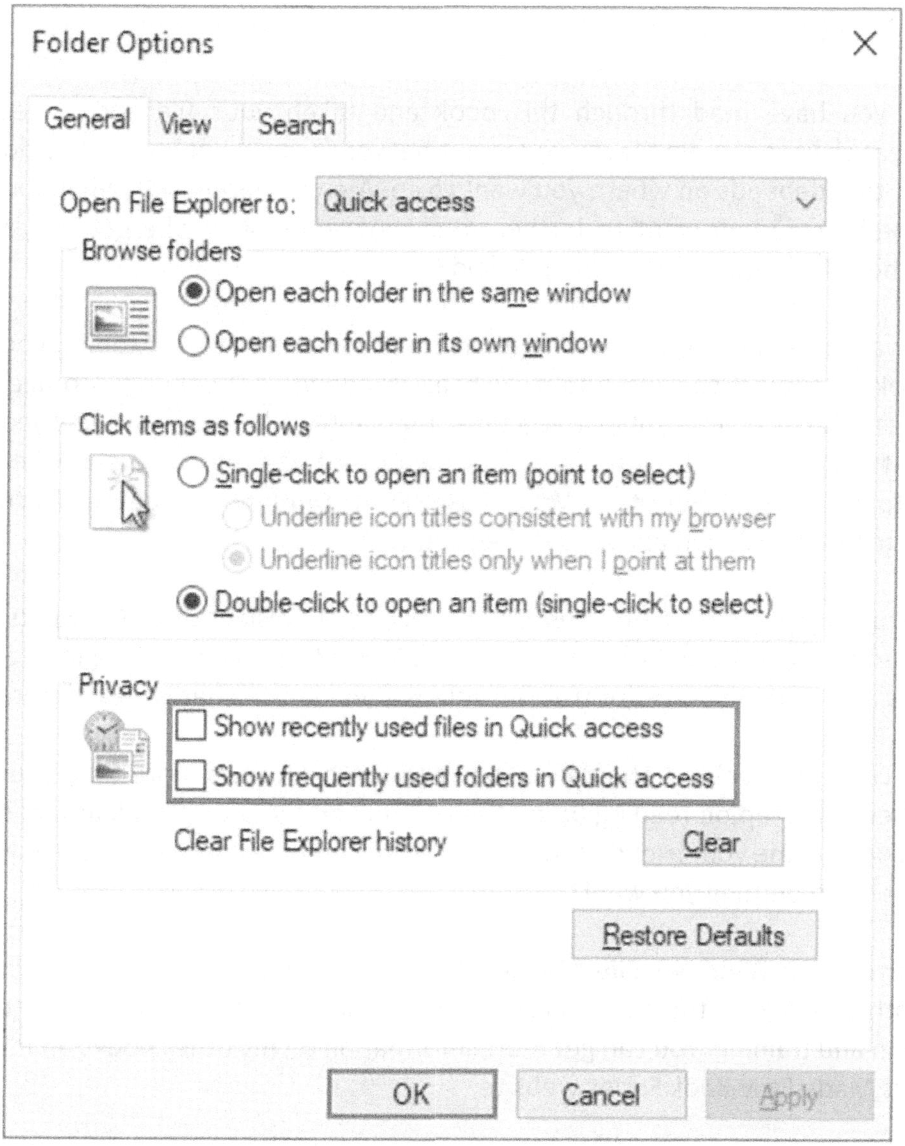

Figure 7.21

Now that you have finished this book, hopefully you have a much better understanding of how important it is to be able to manage your files and folders and how much it really will help you in your day to day computer usage. Like I mentioned before, having this knowledge is essential to be a proficient computer user and they are definitely needed if you want to take your skills to the next level!

What's Next?

Now that you have read through this book and taken your file and folder management skills to the next level, you might be wondering what you should do next. Well, that depends on where you want to go. Are you happy with what you have learned, or do you want to further your knowledge or maybe get into a career in the IT (information technology) field?

If you do want to expand your knowledge on other computer-related topics, you should look at subject-specific books such as Windows, networking, storage, software, etc. Focus on one subject at a time, then apply what you have learned to the next subject. You can also check out my other book that covers a wider range of topics called **Computers Made Easy: From Dummy to Geek** to learn about the topics mentioned above and then some.

There are many great video resources as well, such as Pluralsight or CBT Nuggets, which offer online subscriptions to training videos of every type imaginable. YouTube is also a great source for training videos if you know what to search for.

If you are content in being a standalone power user that knows more than your friends, then just keep on reading up on the technologies you want to learn, and you will soon become your friends and family's go-to computer person, which may or may not be something you want!

Thanks for reading **Windows File Management Made Easy**. You can also check out the other books in the Made Easy series for additional computer related information and training. You can get more information on my other books on my Computers Made Easy Book Series website.

https://www.madeeasybookseries.com/

You should also check out my computer tips website, as well as follow it on Facebook to find more information on all kinds of computer topics.

www.onlinecomputertips.com
https://www.facebook.com/OnlineComputerTips/

About the Author

James Bernstein has been working with various companies in the IT field since 2000, managing technologies such as SAN and NAS storage, VMware, backups, Windows Servers, Active Directory, DNS, DHCP, Networking, Microsoft Office, Exchange, and more.

He has obtained certifications from Microsoft, VMware, CompTIA, ShoreTel, and SNIA, and continues to strive to learn new technologies to further his knowledge on a variety of subjects.

He is also the founder of the website onlinecomputertips.com, which offers its readers valuable information on topics such as Windows, networking, hardware, software, and troubleshooting. Jim writes much of the content himself and adds new content on a regular basis. The site was started in 2005 and is still going strong today.

Made in the USA
Las Vegas, NV
22 September 2023

77952347R00063